REAL ALASKA

ALSO BY PAUL SCHULLERY

1979   *Old Yellowstone Days* (editor)

1980   *The Bears of Yellowstone*

1981   *The Grand Canyon: Early Impressions* (editor)

1981   *The Orvis Story* (with Austin Hogan)

1983   *American Bears: Selections from the Writings of Theodore Roosevelt* (editor)

1983   *Freshwater Wilderness: Yellowstone Fishes and Their World* (with John D. Varley)

1984   *Mountain Time*

1986   *Theodore Roosevelt: Wilderness Writings* (editor)

1986   *The National Parks* (editor and coauthor with Freeman Tilden)

1986   *Wildlife in Transition: Man and Nature on Yellowstone's Northern Range* (with Don Despain, Douglas B. Houston, and Mary Meagher)

1987   *Island in the Sky: Pioneering Accounts of Mount Rainier* (editor)

1987   *American Fly Fishing: A History*

1987   *Bud Lilly's Guide to Western Fly Fishing* (with Bud Lilly)

1988   *The Bear Hunter's Century: Profiles from the Golden Age of Bear Hunting*

1988   *A Trout's Best Friend* (with Bud Lilly)

1991   *Pregnant Bears and Crawdad Eyes: Excursions and Encounters in Animal Worlds*

1991   *Yellowstone Bear Tales* (editor)

1991   *The National Park Service: A Seventy-fifth Anniversary Album* (with William Sontag and Linda Griffin)

1995   *Yellowstone's Ski Pioneers: Peril and Heroism on the Winter Trail*

1995   *Bears—Their Biology and Management* (editor, with James Claar)

1996   *Glacier-Waterton: Land of Hanging Valleys*

1996   *Shupton's Fancy: A Tale of the Fly-Fishing Obsession*

1996   *Echoes from the Summit: Writings and Photographs* (editor)

1996   *Mark of the Bear: Legend and Lore of an American Icon* (editor)

1996   *The Yellowstone Wolf: A Guide and Sourcebook* (editor)

1997   *Yellowstone's Northern Range: Complexity and Change in a Wildland Ecosystem* (with Norman A. Bishop, Francis J. Singer, and John D. Varley)

1997   *Searching for Yellowstone: Ecology and Wonder in the Last Wilderness*

1999   *Royal Coachman: The Lore and Legends of Fly-Fishing*

2000   *Bud Lilly's Guide to Fly Fishing the New West* (with Bud Lilly)

REAL ALASKA

Finding Our Way
in the Wild Country

Paul Schullery

Illustrations by Marsha Karle

STACKPOLE
BOOKS

Published by
STACKPOLE BOOKS
5067 Ritter Road
Mechanicsburg, PA 17055
www.stackpolebooks.com

Printed in the United States of America

10 9 8 7 6 5 4 3 2 1

First edition

Cover design by Caroline Stover

Cover photograph of Brooks Falls bear by Leonard Rue, Jr.

Cover photograph of Brooks River by the author.

Library of Congress Cataloging-in-Publication Data
Schullery, Paul.
    Real Alaska : finding our way in the wild country / Paul Schullery.—1st ed.
       p. cm.
    Includes bibliographical references (p.).
    ISBN 0-8117-0611-7
    1. Natural history—Alaska—Katmai National Park and Preserve. 2. Kodiak
bear—Alaska—Katmai National Park and Preserve. 3. Human ecology.
I. Title.

QH105.A4 S34 2001
508.798'4—dc21   2001020350

For Bill Karle
(1953–2001)

Let us try to find our way. A sojourn in the north country, to see nature at work on the planet's frontier, may give us something to ponder.

—Olaus Murie, *Journeys to the Far North* (1973)

For a time all I knew of the world was a bear shining in the dusk.

—Nick Jans, *The Last Light Breaking* (1993)

CONTENTS

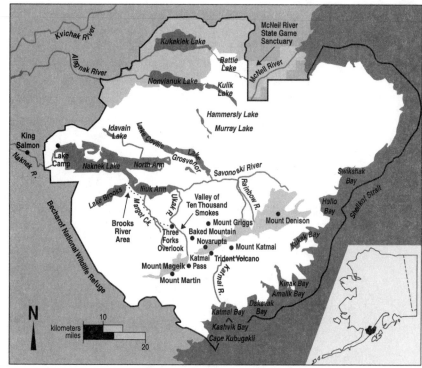

Katmai National Park and Preserve

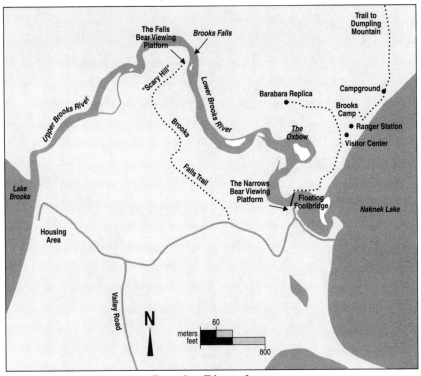

Brooks River Area

Waiting for Alaska

The romance of an adventure hangs upon slender threads.
A banana peeling on a mountaintop tames the wilderness.
—Rockwell Kent, *Wilderness: A Journal of Quiet*
Adventure in Alaska (1919)

In 1959, when I was in sixth grade, I learned about the arctic tern, just the sort of fabulous creature that would appeal to an eleven-year-old boy hungry for ever grander marvels. According to some book that was almost certainly not assigned reading, the arctic tern spent its summers in the Arctic and its winters in the Antarctic, making one of the longest migrations in nature. Like many boys, I was engaged beyond all reason by this kind of Guinness-record performance. I knew just enough geography to imagine the curving hemispheric course of that flight—the epic hardships, the vast rewards of scene and adventure in such a life—but I would give myself too much credit to say I perceived this saga very deeply. I was impressed by the breathtaking extremeness of it, just the way I received the information, at about the same age, that a black ballplayer named Larry Doby had once hit sixty-six home runs in the minors. It called for a specific reassessment of what was possible, a reconsideration of my concept of how things worked. It was my favorite kind of learning, somehow more useful than the genuinely weird platypus-grade wonders, somehow more satisfying than the artificial joys of sports statistics.

Almost forty years later I finally saw arctic terns summering in Alaska. I was on a moving bus in Denali National Park when a tern was pointed out to me as it settled to the shore of a tundra pond, and I took it in with the eyes and emotions of that eleven-year-old. There is a category of delight based on the unanticipated encounter with something known only remotely. When a friend and I, both in our early twenties, first visited Disneyland and walked along its flawless Main Street, and another childhood icon sashayed into view, our unison cry of "There's Mickey!" was uttered with all the spontaneous joy of the five-year-olds around us as we all broke into a run. The tern came to me that way, in a rush of familiarity and unexpected relief after so long a wait that I didn't even realize I had been enduring. Here was not just the animal that of all animals on the planet spent the most of its life in daylight; here was a startling call from my own distant and entirely unarctic childhood. The pond was past and the bird was out of sight before I could do anything more than exult and blabber over my good fortune at finally having such a cherished childhood discovery brought to life.

The next time I saw a tern was along a large glacial lake in Alaska's southeast. Terns darted and swooped about on their midsummer errands along the shore and out over the deep water. Again I enjoyed their acquaintance and rather passively wallowed in nostalgic satisfaction, but then the tern took over. After a moment, one hovered—the first time I'd seen this happen—and everything else about the tern was suddenly trivial. I've watched countless raptors hover as they scanned a meadow for prey, but not until I saw an arctic tern lock itself into place in the sky did I know how a single point in space could define all the rest. The tern rose and appeared to pin its narrow white shoulders to some invisible but microscopically precise set of cosmic coordinates. Watching from below, it seemed for a moment as if all the universe must be slowly revolving around that perfectly stationary little bird. Had I seen two terns do it at once I'm not sure my concept of physics could have stood the shock.

We go to new places in a contradictory mood. We are full of expectations and requirements of things we have been told we must see and check off our list, yet we hope most strongly for the unexpected wonder—for the delight of the tern. Scholars of the sociology, psychology, and history of travel have spent many years sorting out just how our urge to travel works, and, at least to their own satisfaction, they have succeeded. For them, this great quest for the unfamiliar—with its ironic requirement of a familiar with which we can compare it and to which we can return to remember it in comfort—is a matter of considerable ritual. Modern travel, they say, is a tightly prescribed action in which we leave one world and seek another. There is an abundance of cynicism in these analyses, aimed partly at the superficiality of the process but mostly at a prosperous travel industry that for a couple of centuries has been trotting millions of people past thousands of "must-see" attractions in stockyard fashion, just so the hasty visitors can log each wonder in their mental journal of things collected, sights seen, obligations fulfilled. While in Alaska in 1890, John Muir said, "Great is the power of the guidebook-maker, however ignorant."

As a historian of national parks and outdoor sport, I have found these analyses helpful in my work, but I am suspicious of their cynicism. We each react uniquely to the new place or thing, and what we gain from the experience is almost entirely up to inner processes that, though they can be mightily aided by a sensitive guide or terribly handicapped by an inept one, are surprisingly adept at making the most of the moment. If your intellectual and emotional resources are up to it, a long-anticipated glimpse of some ancient Old World wonder from the window of a moving tour bus might turn out to be a high point of your life.

So when I aim the conclusions of the travel scholars at my own experiences, I don't recognize much of use. There is so much more going on here than mere sightseeing. Certainly I still harbor enough of that eleven-year-old boy in my heart to enjoy the new and different and weird, but unfamiliarity is only a matter of degree. Alaska is just past the north end of the same mountain range that I inhabit. It may be different, but it's not the moon. Besides, I travel to lessen unfamiliarity as much as to savor it. I agree with Carl Sagan that our urge to travel was "meticulously crafted by natural selection as an essential element in our survival." Humans move around for very complex reasons. It cheapens what I do to say that when I go somewhere new it's just my desire for novelty that drives me.

People go to Alaska for many reasons. I have heard these reasons either as the people said them, or as I read them, or as I thought I could pick them out as shadowy urges behind other given reasons. Alaska is spectacularly beautiful, hugely overwhelming country. Alaska is fashionable; in certain crowds it is a place (and not all that exotic a place anymore) to add to one's "life list" of destinations from which one has returned. Alaska makes nature almost ridiculously easy to appreciate by just throwing the big, rare things in front of your face in absurd numbers. Alaska's population is skewed to favor women looking for a husband (local sarcasm cautions women that "the odds are good, but the goods are odd"). Alaska invites us to play for a while at Davy Crockett or Robert Service, to act out whatever frontier longing has survived our city upbringing. Alaska, like many other wild places, almost guarantees the receptive soul the most powerful spiritual euphoria available. Alaska is wild; it is, as the song says, "freedom on the run." Alaska is, or was, or likes to pretend it always will be, the last frontier.

Beyond these reasons, Alaska promises the realization of a hundred specific dreams: money; arctic tundra colors to drive a photographer mad; big fish past all imagining and sense; solitude; native crafts so brilliant they settle forever the question of whether craft is somehow less than art; another chance; beautiful animals to adore, study, or shoot, or perhaps all three at once; the simple life; endless wild country to stand in just for the feeling of endless wild country; towns whose names are engraved on our cultural memory but whose appearance we can't even imagine; and, of course and again, money.

At times I've felt the pull of all these attractions and dreams, even the ones I dislike or suspect are unworthy. Waiting for Alaska, I have had plenty of time to sort them out into preferential lists, knowing that if I ever got there the lists would probably have to be thrown out and replaced with new ones.

I don't know when I first began dreaming of going to Alaska. I'm sure that as I grew up, Jack London, Robert Service, and Sergeant Preston were all shaping an idea of the Far North in my head, but I don't recall connecting that image with any plans of my own, mostly because I had no plans. In college in the Ohio Valley in the late 1960s, I was aware of a powerful attraction to the West, but Alaska seemed somewhere off the practical edge of that dream. In 1972 I almost made it there when a friend and I, on the return leg of a fifteen-thousand-mile round-trip from our home in Ohio to Panama, decided that we might as well continue on up the California coast to whatever Canadian town was closest to the southern-most part of Alaska and catch a local flight there, "just to say we did" (another reason for going I didn't list). But I wrecked our car in the Sonoran Desert south of Nogales, and as soon as I'd acquired a new one in Tucson, we hurried home.

By the mid-1970s, after I'd found a way to respond to the attraction of the West and was working as a seasonal ranger in Yellowstone, Alaska had been drawn into my dream life. At first it was there only because so much of the conversation among us young wilderness enthusiasts was about the great battle to save some of Alaska in its wild condition. I distinctly recall announcing to friends that the only ambition I had in my young park service career was that "I want Alaska." But I wanted a lot of other things too, and I eventually took a series of wonderful, fulfilling opportunities that didn't include Alaska. In 1977 I left Yellowstone, spending a few years in Vermont, then in Montana, and then in Pennsylvania. Life went on, and was busy and far richer than I ever imagined it would be.

Then, in 1988, I returned to Yellowstone to work for the National Park Service, where I have since had the honor of witnessing some of modern conservation's greatest struggles and most hopeful milestones, from the fires of 1988 to the restoration of wolves in 1995. In 1996 I married fellow park employee Marsha Karle and have since enjoyed the kind of loving partnership that I had always hoped for but hardly expected to find. Alaska moved further and further back in my mind, pushed out by so many other lucky developments that I could hardly complain, however deep the momentary sadness was when I was reminded of the old dream. I am an inveterate worrier even on these best of days, so missing out on Alaska had to wait in line behind more pressing concerns. I was busy with my park work as an editor, and with my own writing, and Marsha was even busier as Yellowstone's chief of public affairs. I was in my favorite place with my favorite person; how wrong could it be?

Then, late in 1997, Bob Barbee, formerly Yellowstone's superintendent and now regional director of the Alaska national parks, asked Marsha if she'd like to spend some time in Alaska. Bob explained that his public-affairs officer in Anchorage, John Quinley, had come to the job from outside the agency and had missed out on getting practical experience working in a big park. Yellowstone would be good for him. How about Marsha and John exchanging jobs for a while, say six weeks?

Alaska wasn't new to Marsha. Her first job in the park service had been as a secretary in Denali National Park in the early 1980s. She'd moved from there to Yellowstone in 1983, when Bob hired her as his secretary but soon recognized her potential for other things. After a few years in Yellowstone, he packed her off to Denver to work in the park service's regional office, where she became interested in public affairs. With her formidable reserves of cheerfulness and contentment, and her single-minded forthrightness, she was almost ideally suited to the difficult work of spokesperson for the federal government and soon was being given big assignments, leading up to her Yellowstone job. Among many other experiences, she has handled the public-affairs operations for five presidential events in three parks, including the fiftieth anniversaries of Pearl Harbor and Mount Rushmore.

While Marsha considered Bob's invitation, I became aware of a renewal of the old conviction that I simply have to go to Alaska. All at once, right then, Alaska came back to the top of all my lists. And I knew I had waited far too long.

Then Marsha said that this invitation sounded good to her, but a lot of details would have to be worked out. Having spent two long, dark Alaskan winters chopping firewood, she had a less romantic image of the place than I did, but she was interested, partly because during her previous stay there she couldn't afford to do anything or go anywhere. She had lived in Alaska but knew it only locally and would love a chance to see more, especially now that we could enjoy it together.

Details were soon worked out. Plans were made, our bosses were consulted, and conversations with John Quinley confirmed that we could just trade houses; we would stay in John and Connie's shady suburban home in Anchorage, and they and their two children were welcome to our house at Mammoth Hot Springs in Yellowstone. Come spring 1998, we would go.

There was one problem. Twenty years before, I had suffered some mysterious ear problem that made flying a miserable, even terrifying experience. I had almost completely stopped flying by 1980 and had spent less than two hours in the air since. And in many conversations with knowledgeable friends and acquaintances over the year, I had been told that you can't do the *real* Alaska unless you fly.

I always had an almost unreasonable love of flying. Back when I could do it, it never became routine. To me, airplane flights, even milk-run commercial trips home for Christmas, were an adventure on the scale of cruising the galaxy with Han Solo. I just loved being up there. Perhaps that was one reason why Alaska appealed to me when I was younger—one didn't fly merely as a hobby or a treat, but as a way of life.

Now, as I was haunted by that old refrain about the "real Alaska" being available only by plane flight, I decided that I would just go ahead and fly anyway, and hope for the best. There must be drugs, or something, that would make it easier. Meanwhile, I studied the road atlases and was comforted to discover that I could see huge amounts of relatively real Alaska even if I never left my car. It was almost deliriously obvious to me that I could have a sensational experience just by driving to some selection of the places I had heard about for so long: Denali, Seward, Fairbanks, Homer, Valdez, Eagle, Chicken, Tok, Prudhoe Bay. These names and many others were all connected by roads. Just the recitation of the names raised my spirits so much, seemed like such a wondrous invitation to the unreachable, that I immediately went into that stage of pretrip jitters so well described by John Steinbeck in one of the great American road books, *Travels with Charley:* "In long-range planning for a trip, I think that there is a private conviction that it won't happen."

I was relieved of worrying about the long flight from Montana to Anchorage because the foremost corollary to my dream of going there was that I might finally drive the Alaska Highway. The long road through Canada beckoned to me as the last great drive I hadn't yet made in North and Central America. The Yukon had as much appeal—as much seductive magic—as did Alaska.

Because Marsha's work schedule wouldn't allow her the time to drive with me, we decided that I would leave on my drive a couple weeks early. Henry Shovic, a U.S. Forest Service friend from nearby Bozeman, Montana, agreed to take time off in late May and make the drive with me. Henry, a determinedly hopeful man in his late forties with just the kind of quirky sense of humor needed on a trip like this, is a soil scientist with a special interest in landforms and their analysis, which was also just the kind of background I was sure would be most handy on a long trip through unfamiliar country. We would take two weeks. I would drop Henry off in Fairbanks, where he had some Forest Service business to do before flying home, and I'd drive on to Anchorage just in time to pick Marsha up at the airport the day before her work started. Then she would do her work while I went exploring by road. We would share shorter trips on her days off.

Even readers with limited experience as a spouse will recognize the inequity of this arrangement—you work and I'll play—and we did struggle some with it. I tried to correct for my unseemly good fortune by coming home to mow the lawn and do as many other unpleasant things as might even up the score, but I still came out way ahead in time spent doing really great things. It also helped that I soon discovered some research projects that interested me, and I spent more time than I'd anticipated in Anchorage, exploring its wonderful libraries and museums.

Bob had told us right from the start that he might need Marsha to make an official visit to one of the backcountry parks. (In Alaskan parlance, the backcountry is the "bush.") We decided that if that happened, we'd pay my expenses and I'd go along. If possible, while we were already at whatever park it turned out to be, she'd take a few days off so we could spend more time in the "real Alaska." This prospect, though most exciting, again raised the specter of flight, so I talked with my doctor about it. He prescribed some substantial tranquilizers, which I tested by hiring a local pilot to fly me over Yellowstone one day. They seemed to work, sort of. Though I never really relaxed my grip and still tensed with every bump, I had quite a few of the old Han Solo moments as well, alternating between anxiety and exhilaration. Relaxation was out of the

question, but it was an encouraging first try. All my Alaska
flights went well enough, though only the shortest little hops
in float planes were purely fun. They were all pretty much
like that first one over Yellowstone—thrilling and frightening
by turn, too long and yet too short.

Going through these unusual preparations reminded me
that the great internal paradox of the Alaskan wilderness is
that it is in fact so accessible. Driving the Alaska Highway
seemed—and still seems, now that I've done it—a great
adventure, but it was an adventure that Henry and I shared
with a hundred thousand others that year, many of them
retired people rumbling along in huge motorized condo-
miniums. There are plenty of people living a frontier-type life
in remote corners of Alaska. There are plenty of others very
nearly living such a life just outside some Alaskan town
(another favorite local sarcasm is that "the great thing about
Anchorage is that it's only forty-five minutes from Alaska").
But many of those remotely located, hardy souls live with the
jarring reality that any day they may bump into a little flock
of freshly powdered tourists just off a boat or a float plane—
people with every expectation of being back in a comfortable hotel that night. About fifteen years ago, after my father
died, my mother, a retired elementary schoolteacher with an
adventurous spirit, launched a globe-trotting career with various tour groups. She has now been to all seven continents,
most several times. On some of these trips, she has been not
only to Anchorage, Juneau, Fairbanks, and Denali, but also to
Nome, Kotzebue, and the Pribilofs.

I suspected all along that the talk about a "real Alaska"
was untrustworthy anyway. I had heard that sort of mild
chauvinism before, clear across the opinion scale, applied to
my own neighborhood. ("National parks aren't the *real* West,

you know," or "National parks are the only *real* West left, you know.") In judging a place on the basis of its relative "realness," we are typically guilty of at least a little self-promotion. The most "real" place tends to be the one that we either favor ourselves or are more familiar with than the person to whom we describe it, thus establishing a comforting authority for ourselves. More often, the "realness" of a place is the product of other kinds of even more suspect promotion. Tour businesses certainly want you to regard their services as most certain to get you to the *special* places rather than all those shallow, trashy attractions that lesser human beings must settle for, and they will play on your insecurities about missing the genuine article to convince you. We have real rangers on our boats; we'll get you closer to the puffins/bears/totem poles; we'll take you to the stores with the genuine native crafts, not that imitation stuff.

In reading many, many books, articles, and scientific papers about Alaska, fiction and nonfiction, I have yet to find one that does not seem to tell me about real places and people. As diverse a crew of naturalists, historians, explorers, novelists, and journalists as Mardy Murie, Charles Sheldon, Henry Poor, Frank Norris, Robert Weeden, Melody Webb, John Holzworth, Nick Jans, Rex Beach, Sumner MacLeish, Hudson Stuck, Sue Henry, John McPhee, Theodore Catton, James Michener, Velma Wallis, Robert Griggs, John Haines, and many other commentators, all seem to be telling me about Alaskan places it would be naive and rude to describe as anything less than vividly real.

Take Anchorage, the part of Alaska most often singled out for its lack of realness. Novelist John Straley describes its urban distinctiveness as suggestive of something very Alaskan:

Anchorage grew up too fast to keep pace with its ability to dress itself. Today its buildings mostly resemble monumental subarctic toasters, all reflective surfaces to steal the beauty of the surrounding landscape.

Anchorage is hip deep in the twentieth century. In a downtown bar you can find a deranged redneck watching a Rams game on the wide-screen TV alongside an arts administrator who is working on a production of *Waiting for Godot* to tour the arctic villages. Both of them will walk around the Eskimo man bundled up asleep on the sidewalk, but the arts administrator will feel an ironic sense of history.

As I drove in and out of Anchorage, I perceived no edge where the phony ended and the genuine began. One day, as I was entering the Barnes & Noble bookstore, I turned to see a small, dark man in a fatigue jacket approaching; I gave the door enough of a push to ensure that it was open when he reached it and went on in. A few minutes later, sitting at a window seat in the coffee shop, I looked up from my croissant sandwich to see him rooting around for something to eat in the garbage can by the front door; he wasn't interested in books. Not all of Alaska may present just the image we prefer or hope for, but it's something worse than silly to label any of it nonreal.

That's not quite what the "real Alaska" boosters are doing, of course. The best intentioned of them are trying to guide you to what they believe is the place and experience most characteristic of the Alaska they think is most worthy of your admiration. The quest is for authenticity, a quality far more elusive than most casual travelers realize. Alaska never stopped testing my sense of the authentic, and this book is, more than anything else, the results of that test.

For my friends in the conservation business, and for me much of the time—when I can tear myself away from the libraries and museums, anyway—the preferred Alaskan experience leans heavily to wild country with minimal evidence of human presence. The pale rose and lavender tints on the dorsal fin of an arctic grayling I caught after hiking half a mile from the road were certainly no more glorious than the ones on a grayling I caught while standing in the shadow of a Richardson Highway bridge abutment, but context was undeniably important to me.

I went to Alaska with strong feelings about which of the many Alaskan realities most interested me. I knew a lot about wild country and wild things. I knew more than I wanted to about what threatens them, and about the long and sometimes vicious struggle to protect them, and I knew why the battle meant so much. I also knew how to leave the battle behind for a while and just appreciate the gifts of wild country. I had many of the instruments of that appreciation—a formidable past experience, binoculars, field guides, cameras, fly rods, book learning, and an insatiable eagerness—at my disposal. I wasn't starting from scratch in a truly new place. I could tell from my first glances what I had already figured out from my reading about Alaska: It was an extension of places and things I knew well. All I had to do was pay attention to the differences.

I was canoeing and fishing the shoreline of a small lake near Talkeetna one day, discovering yet again that I was nowhere near the canoeist or angler I would need to be to do both at once, when there was a sudden rustle in the grass along the shoreline about a hundred feet from me. It soon turned into thrashing—something was violently disturbed in there right then—and I experienced an entirely unexpected thrill of anticipation, even fear, as I watched. The grass was not two feet tall, but back home I had seen five-hundred-pound animals suddenly rise from such modest cover. I was pretty sure there could be nothing dangerous there, but I couldn't be positive; after all, this was Alaska.

Finally, a large shorebird, similar to a rail but probably something else, waddled out of the grass to the water, where it ignored my passing, my noisy paddling, and my errant fly casts. The great advantage—nothing short of a blessing, really—that Alaska gave me was a chance to learn all the subtle ways in which things that were fundamentally familiar to me could drift over into the unfamiliar. The hover of the tern was repeated in a hundred ways in a hundred other Alaskan moments. An extravagantly pelaged fox I spotted from a rise in the Denali tundra was in sight for only a moment, but like the tern, it completely overhauled a long-held notion of mine; the notion that foxes are a beautiful color became the notion that foxes can make all beautiful colors seem like variations on the same color.

The height of this binge of revised familiarities came when Marsha and I made our hoped-for backcountry trip. We flew southwest from Anchorage, at the head of Cook Inlet on the southern coast of Alaska, to the upper end of the Alaskan Peninsula. We landed at King Salmon, as rawly real a little Alaskan town as you'll find. There we caught a float plane to Brooks Camp in Katmai National Park, where she had to be in attendance during a dignitary's visit, but then could take a few days off and stay on.

For about a week, facts, attitudes, and practices I had come to regard as old friends in my explorations of wild country got a vigorous working over. Moments and episodes from the rest of the summer made a little more sense, or at least had a kind of fit with the new things I was seeing. The "real Alaska" became for me a world that was eerily similar to my own, yet as strangely different and perfect as if the world I knew was just something I had imagined.

Going Ashore

*Few things provoke like the presence of wild animals. They
pull at us like tidal currents with questions of volition, of
ethical involvement, of ancestry.*

—Barry Lopez, *Arctic Dreams* (1986)

Naknek Lake, which is about fifty miles long, is said to be
the largest lake entirely enclosed in an American
national park. Brooks River flows into the lake near the long,
southeasterly trending Iliuk Arm. The big float plane unloaded
our little group of tourists and park staff onto the beach in the
late afternoon. In both directions, the narrow beach curved
out to rounded points, enclosing a half-circle bay in this arm
of the lake. The mouth of the Brooks River was a few hundred yards down the beach to the south of us, but the flat
topography offered little visual proof of that. The beach was
bordered by a low, two-tone forest—a light background of
birches, alders, and other deciduous trees dotted and banded
by stands of darker spruce. Most of the buildings at Brooks—
the small lodge, its cabins and utility buildings, the various
National Park Service administrative buildings, and the housing for lodge and park service staff—are strung along this
shore of the lake, just a short way back in the woods. They are

low wooden or log structures, relatively well suited to a national park setting where human developments are supposed to blend in rather than advertise themselves. Many of these buildings, including the visitor center, are close enough to the lake that they can be seen from the beach through gaps in the woods.

We were promptly directed by our pilot and a waiting ranger to hurry to the visitor center for the orientation required of all visitors to the Brooks River area, but Marsha and I paused long enough for an obligatory photograph of me holding up one end of the huge set of lichened moose antlers that lay in the brush by the Katmai National Park sign. (Looking at this picture now, I recognize it as the first of many from that week to feature the smile I reserve for the most astounding of experiences, in which exhilaration is slipping over into unrestrained goofiness.)

At the visitor center—a cozy little log building—we met the other members of the park service party Marsha was accompanying. They had arrived in another plane that landed over on Brooks Lake, a mile or so to the west on the other side of the narrow isthmus that separated the two lakes. From my map learning, rather than from anything I'd seen on our flight in, I knew that Brooks River flowed in a meandering arc from Brooks Lake to Naknek Lake. It was little more than a mile and a half long from source to mouth.

At the visitor center, some of us sat on benches, some stood. As the orientation lecture began, I edged covetously toward the book sales shelves, immediately identifying a few choice items I hadn't seen in Anchorage bookstores. I knew this orientation was very important; every visitor to Brooks went through it before being allowed to see or do anything else. But I also knew a lot about the routines of bear country, so I found myself listening with an ear not just to learning but to comparing notes. Each national park or forest that is compelled to educate its visitors about bears takes a slightly different tack, once in a while with a major foray away from convention. I am always curious about bear etiquette and how it is shaped by the local bears and the temperaments of the local managers. I therefore listened to the talk and the video with a kind of informed detachment—absorbing the words, recognizing some familiar phrases, raising my eyebrows at interesting rhetorical twists, and, above all else, sensing an intensity of purpose unlike anything I'd encountered elsewhere in the national park system. In any lower-forty-eight park, most of the people who sit through a bear-education talk will probably not even see a bear. But the underlying message coming through here in the visitor center at Brooks was one of urgent immediacy: This is a sure thing, so listen up. You *will* see bears, they may be *very* close to you, and you need to be damn careful out there.

The ranger-naturalist cheerfully conveying this information was Monte Crooks, a stout, mustachioed, middle-aged man who presented his message with the evangelistic vigor of the classic old-style park naturalist. Monte and his video quickly covered the basics. Don't even *think* about carrying food around with you; it goes in the high cache—a miniature log "cabin" on log stilts, with a ladder up to the door—just across the trail from the visitor center. This includes the candy bars in your pockets; *all* food stays here. If you're hungry, get your food bag from the cache and eat right there, at the picnic tables under the cache. Make noise wherever you go, so you never surprise a bear. Clap, sing, talk—the more noise, the better. Stay at least fifty yards from any bear, and if it's a sow with cubs, make it a hundred yards. Right outside the visitor center, there's a little sign on a tree that tells you that you're exactly fifty yards from the life-size brown-painted wooden bear silhouette you can see down the trail by the ranger station. This will give you some idea of how far fifty yards is and how big a bear looks at that distance. If you fish, when you catch a salmon you want to keep (I perked up here, because catching was made to seem like a probability, if not a certainty), you must immediately stop fishing, put the fish in one of the plastic bags provided, and hurry it to the ice house for storage. No lingering to show it off and brag, no streamside cleaning of the fish; *go right now.* If you are playing a fish and a bear comes by, break the line; don't risk feeding that fish to the bear, which will learn to approach other fishermen for similar rewards. If you surprise a bear on a trail, don't run. Talk reassuringly, wave your arms, clap your hands, back away slowly. Monte provided all the quick basics visitors needed to get started in enjoying the Brooks area, but it was mostly about the bears and how to get along with them.

Most of this I recognized as sound and fundamental advice for grizzly country anywhere, but the exceptions were notable. In Yellowstone or Glacier, for example, fifty yards would have been a lot less distance than I would ever recommend. But the overall effect of the orientation was only to raise my anticipation another couple of notches. If I hadn't been excited enough by the low-elevation float-plane ride up the Naknek River drainage from King Salmon and by the prospect of actually being here, hearing in Monte's spiel many implications about how real the local bears were took up any emotional slack I might have had.

I had first heard about Brooks, and about Alaska's other famous bear-viewing areas, more than twenty years earlier, when working on a book about the bears of Yellowstone, published in 1980. Though the book was successively improved by two revised editions, that first try did me the great favor of acquainting me with most of the published bear literature. Insecure about writing a book on bears without being a biologist, I overcorrected by searching out every book and scientific paper I could find on North American bears. As I wrote and edited more books, including several others on bears, the extraordinary situations under which people were seeing Alaskan brown bears assembled at salmon streams became a kind of implausible truth I held off to the side of more conventional knowledge. All this was happening, I knew, but, like the arctic tern's migration, it was only pleasant intellectual freight until I saw it for myself.

I had read and heard most about the tremendous congregations of coastal brown bears at McNeil River, located in a state-run sanctuary on the east coast of the Alaskan peninsula just north of Katmai National Park, but I gradually realized that the most spectacular photographs I saw published were often taken at Brooks Falls, which was somewhere just out the door of this visitor center. It was here, for example, that Tom Mangelsen took his magnificent and exquisitely timed photograph (published, among other places, on the cover of the book *Images of Nature*) of a large brown bear leaning out from the lip of a waterfall, his mouth wide open and about to receive a chrome-bright salmon, caught broadside in mid-leap, its head only inches from the bear's teeth.

But it wasn't until the early 1990s that Brooks came into focus for me as a specific place, with a specific ecological and social context. In 1991 U.S. Forest Service biologist and friend Jim Claar and I were asked to serve as coeditors of the proceedings of the ninth conference of the International

Association for Bear Research and Management. Known, somewhat dyslexically, as the IBA, this is the world organization for bear professionals, whose triennial conferences offer eager bear enthusiasts an overwhelming richness of new information. This particular conference, held in Missoula, Montana, in February 1992, was the biggest yet. Jim, I, and a flock of helpful assistant editors turned all those papers into what I suppose was, at the time of its appearance in 1994, the largest single volume of bear science ever published.

This monolithic document included an engaging paper by two Utah State University researchers, Tamara Olson and Barrie Gilbert (a name I recognized because he had also done work in Yellowstone): "Variable impacts of people on brown bear use of an Alaskan river." The paper reviewed hundreds of hours of observations they had made of Brooks River brown bears and the humans who wandered around looking for bears or, like the bears, fishing for salmon. That paper, and additional publications and eventually even some nature television, made me more aware of specifically what went on at Brooks, but I knew that nothing so indirect could fully prepare me for being there. I really needed to see bears.

At the conclusion of the orientation, Monte gave each of us a "Katmai School of Bear Etiquette 1998" pin with the date on it. We were expected to wear these during our stay. A second pin, a "brown bear booster" pin, was available and distributed to about ten percent of the visitors, those seen behaving especially well. It seemed to me the model of a pleasant, affirmative, and well-aimed educational and preventive law enforcement program, and apparently it makes a big difference, keeping people reminded of how important their behavior is. In 1999 Mark Wagner, Brooks Camp's National Park Service manager, who originated the whole booster program in 1992, added another incentive: a series of collectible cards with color pictures of a local bear and a well-written interpretive message. These, too, are handed out to visitors who are seen taking the bear message seriously. By the time I pinned my bear etiquette pin on my cap, I was more than anxious to have a chance to take the message seriously. Now we'll see the bears, right?

But the park service group to which I was loosely attached decided that it would be grand if we went right over to the lodge and had dinner. What with Alaska's long summer days, they agreed, we would have plenty of time to look around after we ate. I was later to realize that just going from one building to the next at Brooks was ample opportunity to get firsthand bear experience, but of course, none were in sight as we ambled up a short trail to the lodge, filled our plates from the generous dinner trough, and settled around a table.

There was quite a group at this table. Besides Marsha and me, it included National Park Service director Bob Stanton, National Park Service regional director Bob Barbee, Katmai National Park superintendent Bill Pierce, one or two other park service people, and an advance aide for Alaska Senator Ted Stevens, who was to arrive momentarily. It was the director's first visit to Alaska; under Bob Barbee's expert guidance, he was being whisked to so many key park service sites that in only a few days he would see more of the state than my mother has.

In keeping with the tradition established by nearly all previous Alaska legislative delegates, Senator Stevens and the National Park Service have a long and adversarial relationship, so these people were serious and busy in their discussions during dinner. As was true with every major issue at every other national park, any two or more involved parties could be counted upon to represent strongly opposed feelings.

Statehood—especially the part where you're supposed to think of yourself as part of some bigger, national entity—rests uneasily on the shoulders of many Alaskans, whose local interests are superbly championed by their congressional delegations. But in the necessary process of settling federal land-management controversies, these delegations do work hard, and so do the American public's representatives in the land-management agencies. It often is painful to all parties, but they usually manage to come to terms.

The largely bureaucratic dinner conversation (the senator's schedule, details of an inholding controversy, budgeting questions) was characterized by a complete disregard for my agitated state. Nobody seemed to share my need to go see bears. It was one of those self-conscious moments in a trip when you become aware of the whole enterprise as a surprisingly fragile process, a work in progress that can get derailed, or at least lose momentum, long after it has safely survived Steinbeck's early-stage worry that it won't even happen.

For solace, I had to call upon my knowledge of the experiences and lessons of another traveler, the most patient and yet somehow successful of all such anxious adventurers in Alaskan history. Georg Steller was a Bavarian-born naturalist who in the 1730s formed the personal ambition of joining the Russian Vitus Bering on his expedition to explore the *Bolshaya Zemlya,* or "Great Land," which would eventually become known as Alaska. Steller endured ten years of political jockeying, preparatory hardships, brutally difficult travel the breadth of Russia, and finally, one of the most violently arduous sea voyages in the history of scientific exploration, all in hopes of making the kinds of discoveries many young naturalists dream of. But once near the Alaskan shore, Captain Commander Bering proved to be a fanatically timid explorer, dreading mishaps so greatly that he hesitated to approach any shore, much less let his men touch ground. Steller was treated to and tormented by the sight of various Alaskan islands going by just out of reach. For all his pains, all his ten years of preparation, Steller spent a total of ten hours ashore doing his actual natural history work. And yet his name is universally recognized among modern nature enthusiasts, who are amazed to discover that he identified so many species and defined so much of the biological character of Alaska in such a short time. So, however Steller may have felt about his experience in the Great Land, I could only take his example as proof that I, with more than two Alaskan months at my disposal and no ambitious personal agenda for taxonomic immortality, should do all right in a week here at Brooks.

The moment of first arriving at some long-yearned-for destination is an important and almost cathartic step in the journey. Like Steller, we must at least get ashore; once we're there, once we've made our first contact with whatever it is we seek (like Armstrong and Aldrin promptly taking a "contingency sample" of moon soil and placing it in a space-suit pocket so that they would at least have that if they had to abort the mission and lift off), the pressure eases and our perspective shifts and calms. Getting my picture taken with the moose antlers by the park sign had not fulfilled this need; I had not seen bears, or fished for salmon, or done any of the other essential things, so I wasn't really here yet. Most people in the lodge dining room right then could have told me that my contingency sample was a sure thing, but it was my contingency, not theirs, and such assurance is not really transferrable. I wasn't merely waiting through dinner; I had been waiting half my life. By the time we left the dining room and set off for Brooks Falls, I had achieved a rare higher state of readiness. It appeared that the captain commander was finally about to let me go ashore.

The trail south from the lodge parallels the lakeshore, but it stays in the woods, passing the small store, the fish-storage shack, and another outbuilding or two, then emerging from under the low forest canopy at the north shore of Brooks River, right where that stream meets the lake. A narrow, softly bobbing pontoon bridge with a sturdy pipe railing crossed the river just upstream from its wide mouth. From the bridge, I got my first look at the local fishing scene. There were a few fly fishermen wading here and there in the river, some in the narrow deep bend upstream of the bridge, a few out in the fanning currents closer to the lake, but none were visibly successful right then.

Across, where the bridge touched the south shore of the river, there was a long, elevated wooden platform from which park staff and visitors watched for the putative bears. The platform was a curiosity for me. Partly obscured by small trees, fronting the shore of the river just where it broadens and transforms itself from a flow to a bay, the platform was a long, doglegged wooden affair with stairs on one end and a handicap-access ramp on the other, both leading up to the railed viewing area about ten feet above the ground. Both the stairs and the ramp were gated with simple wooden gates such as you would expect at the front of any fenced yard. I was beginning to sense the differences between this place and my Yellowstone home more keenly now. It was obvious that the elevated wooden platform was regarded as a sanctuary for people. And unless the local rangers were using magic bear-warding spells on those flimsy gates, the only imaginable explanation for this improbable arrangement was that the antifood discipline enforced on park visitors was almost perfectly successful. Any bear that wanted to go up there on the platform and look around was not going to be stopped by the gates, so no bear must ever want to.

Beside the platform, there was the start of a gravel road that headed back into the forest on a course more or less parallel with the south side of the river. This road continued on across the isthmus to Brooks Lake, with a side road to the Valley of Ten Thousand Smokes, but we didn't go that far. After a few hundred yards, we came to a trail that led off into the mottled shade of the spruce forest on the right, back toward the river.

On the trail, Bill Pierce, our leader, immediately established himself as the kind of man I most like to hike with in bear country. With vigilant regularity, his conversations were punctuated by handclaps that carried like small-caliber gunshots, and his frequent calls to the bears boomed and echoed in the woods. To this authoritative accompaniment, we wound through a flat forested bottomland, a still, low-elevation white spruce forest with a mixture of familiar and unfamiliar undergrowth. If Marsha and I could ever relax enough to make this little hike for its own sake, we'd need our field guides to sort out the tiny flowers and shrubs. I noticed kinnikinnick and one or two other probable matches with plants I knew, but it was hard to concentrate on such details. The shrub cover was broken with unnerving frequency by cross-trails that Bill, and Karen Gustin, the park service manager of the Brooks area, assured us were created and maintained entirely by the bears that I still knew only as large, carnivorous rumors.

Leaving the spruce forest behind, we climbed a low, hummocky ridge into a sparse birch wood. A ranger later told us that the ridge was known informally as "Scary Hill."

We followed the ridge, which was oddly lumpy and pocked with shallow depressions, to the river.

As the trail descended from the sunny top of Scary Hill, it reentered the birch-alder-willow woods that solidly walled both sides of the stream. When still well back from the river and perhaps fifteen feet above the river's level, the trail ended at another wooden gate, this one featuring a simple sign with the international symbol prohibiting something—the red circle with diagonal slash—in this case, bears. Behind the diagonal slash was a very official-looking silhouette of a bear. No bears allowed. This seemed enormously amusing right then and gave the whole place a fine and slightly desperate comic relief that I came to realize characterized much of the relationship between people and bears here. Opening the gate, Bill and Karen led us along a level ramp, underneath which the slope fell away, until we reached the main viewing platform, a two-level affair that would hold a tightly packed forty standing people. There were about twenty there, all looking out over the river, which at this point was about 150 feet wide, and

the falls, which were about seven feet high. The river flowed into view from the left, dropped over the falls, and continued on down to the right through a long, islanded riffle. The water was visible for hundreds of yards downstream, then bent out of sight into its last curves before reaching Naknek Lake. I only took these peripheral features in later, because there were bears at the falls.

The nearest one, about a third of the way across toward the other side of the falls, was unquestionably posed in the exact spot where Mangelsen's famous bear-and-salmon scene had taken place. Another was just a few feet beyond, like a second image in a mirror. A third was standing below the falls closer to the far shore, perhaps ten feet out from the base of the falling water, staring intently at the foam. Nobody moved; they just stared and waited.

I have learned to be extremely conservative in estimating the sizes and weights of fish and bears. Caution seemed especially important now, with bears standing against a background as unfamiliar as this, where I had nothing to mentally measure their bulk against. I suppose they weighed between four hundred and five hundred pounds, but that was a conservative guess. It was early in their feeding season, and I assumed they would get much larger by the end of the year if they got a lot of fish. By local standards, they were lean, just beginning the big summer and fall feeding binges that would prepare them for hibernation, but I could not call them gaunt. They looked just fine.

Their fishing posture reminded me of my former dog Nellie, a Cardigan Welsh corgi, a breed celebrated for its enthusiasm for action and work. When Nellie crouched and tensed while waiting for me to throw the ball, in that professional grade of concentration dogs reserve for really important things, and her upper lip rolled up a bit in anticipation of a short, furious chase, there seemed to be room for nothing else in her consciousness but the ball. These bears did not seem quite as keyed up as she had, but they were obviously braced for action. This was strictly business. Occasionally a big head swung slowly to one side or a foot would shift to better brace the bear against the current.

After a few moments, I realized that their heads seemed differently proportioned than those of the bears I knew—longer and more angular, perhaps. Their ears seemed more pronounced, as well. Though neglected by almost all the many writers who have commented on why bears reach so successfully into so many corners of the human imagination, bear ears are an important part of what makes the animal so appealing. Imagine how different the bear would look to us, and how different would be our reaction to the sight of it, if its ears were pointed like a fox's, or droopy like a hound's. Those little rounded ears, with their almost tacked-on presentation toward the top and well back on the head, have contributed greatly to the bear's enormous range of personality in human culture. Small and neutral enough in shape to be cute when we needed cuteness, the ears were inconsequential when fury was called for. Try to imagine a cottontail rabbit with its eyes aflame with rage and its lips drawn back in a vicious snarl; even if you succeed in imagining the rage and the snarl, the big perky ears will ruin the effect.

Brooks bears, at least the few big males that dominated the best spots at the falls that week, brought something new to the whole ear issue. Once noticed, it distracted me all week. For the size of the animal, I doubt that they were out of proportion, but through some combination of color and shape, they were immediately more noticeable. The bear ear is not a flat flap; it curls around the ear opening. Perhaps because they were a few shades lighter in color than the head, and because that lighter shade caught the light so well (on sunny days, they were almost bright), they became an added attraction in my enjoyment of the animal. They looked like big, furry softballs glued on there. They were irredeemably cute.

Cuteness wasn't among my primary expectations here, nor is it an impression that bear managers like to see encouraged among park visitors. Cautious respect or outright awe was more in keeping with the mood of the place. These were the famous "coastal brown bears" I had read about for so long. They gather at salmon streams all along the upper Alaskan peninsula and on east around the southern and southeastern Alaskan coast, as well as on some of the larger islands near shore. Those populations blessed with runs of the largest salmon, such as the bears of Kodiak Island, may weigh twelve hundred pounds or more after a good summer.

They are called brown bears, but they are not a different species than the grizzly bear. Wherever they live and whatever they eat, they are all—from the grizzly bears in Yellowstone, to the Toklat grizzly bears of Denali, to these Brooks

River bears, and all across Russia and Europe to the shy little grizzly bears of Italy's Abruzzo National Park—part of one remarkably variable species, *Ursus arctos*. (The Kodiak giants are a distinct subspecies.) As Andy Russell observed in his essential classic, *Grizzly Country* (1967), if a male coastal brown bear encounters a female interior grizzly bear, "he does not pause to thumb through the social register before taking her for a mate." The bears I saw here at Brooks Falls were, for practical biological purposes at least, just my neighborhood bears back home after many thousands of years of adaptation to a different and very hospitable environment. Or, to get the chronology right, my neighborhood bears were these bears after thousands of years of adaptation to the wildlife-rich interior of western North America. *Ursus arctos,* like the wolf and the human, has a gift for flexibility and a knack for getting by in the most unlikely places.

This flexibility has made it hard to give them a really reliable name. Though some early writers tended to treat "grizzly" and "grisly" as interchangeable terms ("gristly" is another obscure variant) applied to an animal that they thought was both, the grizzly bear was actually named for the "grizzled" mixture of colors or shades in its hair. Some of the longer guard hairs may be lighter or darker than the mass of body hair, and other individual hairs may be tipped in paler shades, thus the popular nineteenth-century name "silvertip." Most of the grizzly bears I've seen in the lower forty-eight had grizzled coats, though a few were a solid color, ranging from a near palomino to a very near perfect black. The effect of the coat's "haloing" with lighter outer hairs is a wonderfully complicated visual impression; you are hard-pressed to tell what color the bear is. Instead of saying it is brown, or gray, or silver, you describe a bear as light or dark, meaning that the overall appearance places it somewhere along a spectrum of relative shades. The advanced observer may notice all sorts of little individualities: lighter shoulder hump, legs, feet, or face. There may be other patchiness around the eyes or snout, and the claws are as variable, with some individuals having nearly white ones and others nearly black. Cubs sometimes have distinct pale collars around their necks. Few other wild animal species—the wolf and fox come to mind—exhibit such a range of variation in how their colors are combined as does the grizzly bear. Many bears undergo surprisingly dramatic changes over the summer as they molt into a darker coat that is then bleached by the sun.

Charles Sheldon, who hunted and studied Denali's bears in the early 1900s, said that the Toklat grizzly bears had grizzled coats when they entered hibernation, but "they all emerge from the winter den with coats of uniform color." The Toklat bears that I saw in Denali in June, though quite grizzled, tended to offer a straw-colored visual effect; one Denali bus driver suggested a very effective mental search image for them by telling her passengers to "look for the little haystacks." All of these individual variations in color and appearance are also subject to almost unbelievable changes that occur when you view the same bear from different angles relative to the sun, in the light of different days, or when the bear is wet or dry.

More than half of the fifteen or so different bears I saw that week at Brooks were at first glance nearly uniform in color. When their coats were wet and the tips of the longer hairs adhered to pull long clumps of hair into hundreds of little points, the coat seemed more contrasty, with the darker undercoat showing through more clearly. Even when dry, a few showed some amount of grizzling, but among the few bears I saw, it seemed far less pronounced than I was accustomed to. Most of the big males that dominated the good fishing locations at the falls were a pale brown, more oak than walnut. Not being fattened up, they did seem to wear their coats a little loosely, but it is part of the physiological reality of the brown/grizzly bear that from some angles it looks a little uncomfortable in its clothes. With its powerfully muscled shoulders humped up, the bear may appear as swaybacked as an old horse, like a heavy wool blanket tossed over a snowmobile.

But once the bear is fattened up, all is massive roundness. A researcher friend who spent a summer along another Alaskan salmon stream said that the brown bears maneuvering through the heavy grass and brush near the stream looked like "a bunch of furry Volkswagens." Later in the week, when I was able to watch the Brooks bears pass directly underneath me on both platforms and get an overhead view I never got (or wanted, because it would mean I was treed by the bear) in Yellowstone, I decided that even early in the year, the brown bear gives new meaning to the term "fullness of being."

Brooks Falls is not straight. It does not break over an even, unbending shelf that runs directly from one bank to the other. Instead, the line of the brink swerves forward and back a couple times. In some places, big dark rocks protrude from the brink, or through the falls themselves. Almost all the way across, the water rushes over the ragged, rocky edge with a rim of smooth, blue-green flow that rushes down into the white of the fall. The pool below the falls is a frothy turmoil of foam and rock, the water roiling around submerged obstacles and churning along for some distance before reorganizing in a flat, dark flow and continuing on downstream. Over the ages, the salmon that run up this stream have found their way to the best holds below the falls, places that provide them sufficient depth and traction to make the furious short burst of speed that will carry them up. Over the same ages, the bears have identified, with great precision, the very best places to stand to intercept those flights. There they stand, knee- or chest-deep in the powerful flow, and there they wait. They have also identified the best places in the foamy turbulence below the falls to watch for other fish swimming by. Generally, bears that can't take and defend the best places on the brink settle for these. Other bears, too low in the hierarchy to earn any of these places, cruise the edges of the stream or adopt more creative strategies that I was to witness as the week went on. But for all the bears that were serious contenders for the good places, it was a matter of getting into position, concer.trating on the source of the salmon, and waiting.

And waiting. We arrived very early in the summer run, so fish numbers would have been fairly low anyway, but the year of our visit was also the second consecutive season in which the Bristol Bay sockeye salmon run was judged a disaster. For whatever combination of reasons, the sockeyes were return- ing in extremely low numbers, which meant that the bears— and those of us watching—were waiting a long time between fish. Sometimes ten or even fifteen minutes would pass before a fish would rocket out of the foam and either flop into the upper part of the falls to be washed back down, make it into the upper river, or meet the lunge of a waiting bear, which often missed. If the bear caught the fish, he immediately vacated his spot and took his prize to shore to eat it. Another bear might or might not try to occupy the empty spot while he was gone.

The overriding biological truth of this scene, the thing that ruled the behavior and thus the excitement of all the bears and humans up and down the river, was that nothing happens unless salmon are there. The more salmon, the more happens. Many salmon, and more happens than can be comprehended. My favorite description of this falls when the salmon are at their thickest is probably the first detailed account of the event in print. It was left by Robert Griggs, the National Geographic Society–sponsored scientist whose series of exploratory expeditions into the Katmai country between 1915 and 1917 led to the creation of Katmai National Monument in 1918. In 1919 his group camped at Brooks River and witnessed what was probably the peak of the run in a good year:

> Here we stood for hours, held by the fascination of one of the most wonderful sights afforded by the animal kingdom, as the endless procession of fish kept leaping high in the air, up and over the falls.
>
> Never did a second elapse between jumps. Sometimes as many as six fish were in the air at once. The jump appeared to require their full powers; none made the attempt except at the lowest notch in the falls, and none jumped clear over in a way to suggest that they could have gone much higher if necessary. Many of the leaps were so wide of the mark as to give the impression that they were not serious attempts, but rather in the nature of reconnaissances—efforts to learn the best place for the ascent. Often the fish struck themselves on the sharp rocks. Among those below the falls were many terribly lacerated by such accidents—so far gone that there

was little probability of their ever succeeding in the leap.

At first we were inclined to think that very few were successful, but careful observation showed that great numbers were getting up. After a number of counts at different times, we estimated that they were ascending at the rate of about 20 a minute, or 1,200 an hour.

Wildlife watching is an act whose rewards are in direct proportion to the watcher's restraint. For some people, it is necessary to get out there and interact with the animal in some way, a need similar to the one I feel when I see fish— I have to do something direct. But most of the time, I believe that the guiding principle of the wildlife watcher should be to require nothing of the animal beyond what it would do if it were not being observed. Unless you are there to hunt the bear—and thereby enter into its world much more assertively, with all the physical and metaphysical risks such entrance entails—all that the bear represents as animal and as citizen of the land should be available for your enrichment without bothering it. Most casual visitors to wildlife reserves exhibit almost childish impatience at the slow pace of things, usually borne of the unrealistic expectations raised by television nature programming in which huge periods of time are compressed into thirty minutes of nearly frenetic action on film. We see the killer whale whapping the bloody seal carcass back and forth on the ocean's surface, but we are given no appreciation for the long intervals of unviolent cruising and resting that occupy so much more of the whale's life (or of the seal's, for that matter). Nature programming that accurately and proportionately depicted the activities of any wild animal would put almost everybody to sleep, and put the broadcasting channel out of business.

That does not excuse us for our impatience, however, when we are confronted with a view of the real animal out in its world. Then we face other challenges and are dependent upon our own resources, rather than the film producers, for success.

But success in watching or appreciating wildlife is not simply measurable, nor is it easily definable. Part of the challenge is in coming to terms with how differently the game is played from one place to the next. Standing there at Brooks Falls, I was in a kind of charmed awe. It was enough for me to have these unmoving bears in view, and to enjoy the quality of their attention: that pure, guileless physical and mental alertness of animals at ease in their environment. But as I watched and wondered, I was also struck by the quality of my own attention and the deceptive simplicity of the scene.

We love the big, wild herbivores—the deer, elk, bison, caribou, and the rest—and nowadays we adore the predators. Brooks Falls makes it so easy to enjoy all this simple-mindedly, because we get to see predation that evokes no empathy. After all, they're "just fish." At Brooks we are usually spared the harder sights of these same bears at different seasons, calmly dismantling a still-bleating caribou calf, or rousting and hastily inhaling a whole family of squirrels. Brooks is in one way ideal for the beginning wildlife watcher because it offers such quick rewards; it gets you hooked on the whole business of observing. But in another way, it slips you into the activity without any warning of the harder emotional dues you will pay if you stay. The sound of the cracking, popping backbone of salmon being fed on by a nearby bear is an early warning of the real show, and of the aesthetic and even spiritual challenges ahead of you if you admit that animals are free to respond to their own evolutionary imperatives rather than our personal moral codes.

Though I have been seriously watching wildlife for more than twenty-five years, I earned most of my skills watching Yellowstone's carnivores over the past ten. Under the tutelage of experts, especially bear biologists Marilynn and Steve French, I became part of a new school of wildlife watchers that has emerged in Yellowstone and a few other western parks. Since bears and other animals have been largely divorced from human foods—from garbage dumps, from motorists, from picnic tables—and have been forced to redistribute themselves where natural foods are most available, wildlife watching has become a far more challenging and rewarding process than it was when our parents and grandparents were lobbing leftovers at roadside black bears and unloading dump trucks of rotting garbage on eager grizzly bears at backcountry "bear pits." We new wildlife watchers have learned what a few naturalists, bird-watchers, and sportsmen have known for generations: Wildlife watching is not a matter of luckily happening upon an animal. It is a matter of understanding the animal, of hard work getting to the right places, and of patience. The understanding and the hard work are fairly straightforward and easy enough to come by; the patience is not.

The new approach took quite a while to catch on and probably never will appeal to most hasty visitors. A few people, like the Frenches, put in hundreds, even thousands, of hours with binoculars and spotting scopes, applying all that science had taught us about how bears behave and what bears eat to figure out where the bears will be and when they will be visible. The result of their example is what amounts to a major new visitor activity in national parks, an activity further heightened and popularized in Yellowstone by the arrival of wolves, which were reintroduced amid enormous controversy and excitement in 1995.

I have my own favorite places for doing this, hills from which I can look out across tens of thousands of acres of wildland. With low-power optics for scanning and high-power optics for closer observation once I've found something, I can find and watch Yellowstone's wild mammals as far as four miles off. At four miles, if you have enough practice, it is still possible to distinguish a black bear from a grizzly and tell a great deal about what it is doing. (With my modest and fairly cheap scope, I've identified bears at six miles, but even in the dry West, there is usually too much heat distortion in such a great stretch of air for any serious observation.)

I'm not a master at this, but I've put in enough hours to be competent and a little proud of my skills. I can recall, after a few years of working on these skills, the first time I took them somewhere else. Marsha and I made a long weekend trip to Glacier National Park, about 350 miles north of Yellowstone. I was already familiar enough with the park to know something about where animals were seen, and I was also familiar enough with the animals that lived there to know where to look for them once I got to a likely spot, but this early-spring trip was the first time I'd gone solely to exercise my skills at spotting things. It went almost too well; everywhere I expected to see something, I did. There are times when nature is so generous you can't help getting an inflated view of your craft (but then the next week nature makes you sit and wait for several days before showing you a single coyote scratching itself recreationally, and you deflate).

This was the frame of mind I brought to Alaska. I saw Alaska partly as a new opportunity to exercise these skills and perhaps show off a little bit, if only for myself.

My first chance was in Denali. There, the National Park Service has established a terrific system for getting visitors out among the wild animals with the least possible effect on the behavior of the animals and the highest possible odds of the people seeing them. An eighty-nine-mile road leads into the heart of the park, and though threatened with "improvements," it is mostly unpaved. Anyone may drive the first fifteen miles, a spectacular enough trip, but the rest of it is open only to a system of tour and shuttle buses that operate on a generous schedule. From these buses, visitors of all degrees of familiarity with wild country and wildlife can enjoy the show. If you want to take a hike or just stand by the road and gawk, the driver will let you off wherever you ask (except close to grizzly bears). Just catch the next bus when you want to continue.

Though I see this as a perfectly reasonable way to manage public use in a national park—indeed, I would like it tried in some areas in the lower-forty-eight parks—by temperament, I am much more a solitary traveler, so I tended to get off the bus and poke around on my own. But when my goal was just to catch a glimpse of as many animals as possible, and to get a feel for the breadth and reach of this great landscape, there was no replacing the buses.

My first experience of the buses was an almost rude affront to my hard-earned skills as a wildlife watcher. That morning, I settled into a front seat in a full bus, recognizing my fifty or so fellow passengers as the usual assortment of park visitors: enthusiastic people from all over, most with very little experience or interest in serious wildlife watching. As we climbed the grade from park headquarters out onto the taiga, with long-distance views in both directions, I noticed a bull moose way off at the base of the hills to the south. I said, "There's a moose over there by the hills," loud enough for the driver to hear, which meant that quite a few other people heard too. This, after all, was how it worked: The whole bus was the spotter, and we were all encouraged to sing out whenever we saw something. The driver, an older man with many years' experience on this route, dutifully slowed, while people got their binoculars and cameras aimed. Some left their seats on the other side of the bus to squeeze in for a look.

When the driver realized how far off the moose was, he announced over his loudspeaker that we would move on and look for something closer. We all settled back down and resumed our watch. After I had done this two or three times, I caught the driver giving me a sidelong, half-annoyed, "Who *is* this guy?" look, which at first I thought was flattering. I got cocky, making a flashy over-the-right-shoulder sighting of a very distant grizzly bear as it climbed through a small patch of bare ground on a high ridge that the bus had already passed. Hardly anyone on the bus could see it up there; those who could were not necessarily able to tell what it was. It was just a tiny brown blob. But I was so excited to be in Alaska seeing bears, and so pleased that I was good at it, that I couldn't help pointing it out.

About the time I saw this bear, it began to soak in that I wasn't really helping. After we left the paved road where all the traffic was, animals were common and often quite close to the road. For the purposes of the Denali bus, my skills were irrelevant and even troublesome.

Worse, I was not only showing off, I was also succumbing to the sort of competitive mood that I always found so distracting among wildlife watchers back home. In any given group of watchers along a road in Yellowstone or Glacier, some people log their sightings like trophies, eagerly scanning the slopes not merely to see the animal, but to see it first. I could feel this urge, especially when other bus passengers, either because they too had skills or because they were just naturally good at this, saw something before I did.

So I shut up. There was so much wildlife to be seen, and so many eager eyes trained on the landscape, that little would be missed. There were Dall sheep, ptarmigan, the occasional caribou, the occasional bear, even a coyote that the driver hopefully agreed was a wolf. It was all a great thrill for me, but I was in one narrow little sense kind of disappointed. This Alaska was a pie in the face of some of the skills I had worked so hard to bring here.

Brooks Falls rubbed it in some more, making my wildlife-finding skills even more thoroughly irrelevant. At least at Denali, I could enjoy the search, scanning the country for wildlife, sorting out all the shades of brown and green, stopping to visually explore especially promising spots more carefully. Here at Brooks, there was no visual search except the one conducted to avoid actually tripping over the bears. It was more like watching birds at a feeder; one's viewing opportunities were more a matter of waiting for animals to show up than of going out and searching for them. Wildlife watching is different without the thrill of the chase.

This first look at Brooks Falls and its bears was memorialized for me by Bob Barbee. As I leaned on the rail in my bear trance, soaking up the sight in simple-minded gratitude, he quietly motioned to Marsha to stand next to me. She obligingly cozied up next to me, and Bob photographed us like that, both looking off into some dreamy distance like those studio pictures of starry-eyed newlyweds pondering their promises.

Shortly after that, we made our way back over Scary Hill, through the forest of bear trails, and on up the gravel road to the park service's small administrative area along the shore of Brooks Lake. Here, two park service men, Jim Gavin and Tom Ferguson, had generously offered us the spare bedroom in their cabin. Jim was the maintenance foreman for the area, and Tom was a heavy-equipment operator who graded the unpaved road from Brooks out to the Valley of Ten Thousand Smokes. Both were tall, lean, and of an unsuppressed cheerfulness about what a wonderful place they got to spend their summers. Our luggage, food, and fishing gear arrived on one of the little three-wheeled Cushman utility vehicles that sped up local transportation at Brooks (picture mutant golf carts with closed cabs and tiny pickup-truck beds). Certain contingencies had been honored, and despite my ecstatic state over what I had just seen and what was before me this week, sleep seemed possible, if only because the drugs I'd eaten for my flights that day were finally taking full effect.

Got 'im

I am living out a dream in these woods.
—John Haines, *The Stars, the Snow, the Fire* (1989)

It was late morning before we were free to go to the falls platform. We reached the trailhead a little before eleven o'clock, and clapped and shouted our way through the spruce forest, then up onto Scary Hill and along its winding, lumpy path through the birches. We made noise the whole way; the people on the platform could surely hear us coming.

I was in front as we came down off the hill. The little gate with its "no bears allowed" sign was directly ahead of us, when I unexpectedly stepped into an old Jimmy Buffett song:

> *That's when I first saw the bear;*
> *he was a big Kodiak-lookin' feller, about nineteen feet tall.*

Under the shady canopy of an old birch just to the right and uphill a little way from the gate, one of the big, light brown bears was standing broadside to us, watching us approach. Later examination of the spot suggested that I was

45

perhaps fifty feet from him right then. Maybe it was more. It seemed like less.

In many years of wandering in bear country, I have seen a number of grizzly bears at various distances in the backcountry, and even surprised a couple that immediately ran off, but I had never found myself face-to-face with one this close. Neither had Marsha. Over those years, I had plenty of time to think about what I would do when this happened. I had read hugely in the scientific and popular literature on bear encounters. I had talked to experts, to people who had had such encounters and walked away, and even to a couple of mauling victims. I had made many miles of noise to avoid such an event. I had absorbed all the advice, considered the odds of each possible tactic working or failing, and developed such habits as could be cultivated, such as being especially careful near noisy stream courses and on windy days, and always keeping an eye out for tracks, scat, diggings, and big, climbable trees.

But I knew that no amount of planning provided reasonable assurance that my personal reaction would be the right one, or even a sensible one. This isn't because the advice wasn't good or because habits aren't worth developing. It is because inside each of us is a different person whom we don't know very well, and that person is just waiting to come out and surprise us with some strange combination of fright, fortitude, common sense, and idiocy when it is finally our turn to meet the bear. "What do you do when you meet one?" had been a favorite bear-related question asked by many of the campers to whom I gave evening campfire programs during my ranger-naturalist days. My stock answer was that I didn't know what *anyone else* was going to do, but I didn't think it would be a problem for me, because I fully expected to faint.

When it finally happened there at Scary Hill, my reaction was, sad to say, much more prosaic than that. Briefly and softly, yet emphatically, I swore. It was entirely involuntary, no thought or creative phrasing involved. I just said, "Oh shit." This caused Marsha to glance up from the rough trail's uneven footing, look past my shoulder, and see the bear too, but her reaction was more restrained. The bear showed no reaction at all.

We stood there only a few seconds before I said, "Let's just walk back." We turned around and moved back up the trail onto the ridge, where the bear was no longer in sight. There we stopped and did as good a job of milling around uncertainly as two people could. We had not seen the bear move the whole time.

The ranger assigned to the platform had been partway along the approach ramp toward the gate and had seen us retreat. What with the intervening foliage, I'm not sure she could see the bear from her angle, but it had to be obvious why we were moving back. Typically the person assigned to the falls platform was in regular radio contact with a counterpart at the platform by the bridge so that they could keep track of how many people were at each place and let each other know if their space was full up or if a bear was somewhere in the way. Our ranger was probably just monitoring traffic, which meant she had to be near the gate.

We were not able to see each other, but we were easily able to call back and forth. We asked her where the bear was. She told us it was now close to the gate. It was still unclear if we should wait here or go back. Then she called that the bear had moved out onto the trail and lain down, which settled the issue. We called that we would come back later and left, clapping and yelling even more energetically.

In Yellowstone or Glacier, this close an encounter would have been a matter of the most dire peril. Such a short distance was well inside the "fight or flight" reaction threshold of most of our larger wild animals, especially in the back-country. (Animals that calmly graze while surrounded by camera-faced tourists along a park road will usually flee from the very sound of approaching hikers the next day a mile from the same road.) All my book learning on grizzly bears suggested to me that at that instant when "I first saw the bear," I was his, and he very possibly would claim ownership. Despite my best efforts to follow the rules, I had messed up—blaming the bear is nonsense—and I was dead meat if the bear wanted to bother with me. So was Marsha.

I am not exaggerating for dramatic effect. I had many years of conditioning to this viewpoint, from people and information sources who knew best. I knew that much, if not most, of the time in such situations, the bear will probably leave (the grizzly bears in the lower forty-eight display incredible forbearance), but I also knew that I had no right to expect such a good break.

But my more recent learning about these brown bears seemed to teach me differently. Encounters like ours, and considerably more intimate ones, were an everyday occurrence at Brooks. People and bears bounced off each other's personal spaces constantly, ricocheting around with an unnerving abandon. I would have more very close encounters with *Ursus arctos* in the next few days than I'd had in the previous twenty-five years.

Before I went to Alaska, a biologist friend had asserted that "that's a different bear up there. It's much more mellow and easygoing." The rationale for this was that these bears were so fat and happy from the ever-flowing larder of the river, and had spent so many hundreds of generations living this good life, that they were a lot harder to alarm. As odd as it sounds to the uninitiated, it is true that most North

American grizzly bear attacks are defensive measures on the part of the bear, usually because a bear has been surprised at too close quarters when it has something it feels it must defend, such as a carcass it is eating or cubs it is trying to raise in a hostile world. All bears everywhere still have these boundaries and will respond to such threats; it's just that the need to respond has been muted in bears like those at Brooks, and they tend to put up with a lot more than my Rocky Mountain bears will before they flee or attack.

Even though I could absorb this information on an intellectual level, I never stopped having trouble with it on an emotional level. My training was too strong. Besides, I knew too much about the bears. The bears at Brooks emerged from their dens long before the salmon started running. Until there were fish to eat, they had to make their living eating other things, some of which were warm-blooded animals that would try to run away. These big bears, as lumbering and benign as they might seem, were no strangers to working hard to acquire prey, and they ate any animal they could get. It helped to rationalize that behavior by comparing it to that of the roadside animals in Yellowstone: While these bears were at Brooks River, with its bounty and its unthreatening human pedestrians, they might behave differently than they did at other seasons and in other places—but they were still bears, and they still looked about nineteen feet tall.

The other difference between these bears and the grizzlies in the lower forty-eight has to do with a very complicated process known as habituation. Habituation occurs constantly in the world of wildlife. Deer that invade your garden are not "tame," though that word is often applied to them, especially the ones that get hand-fed by your neighbor. They have not become domesticated like your house pets have after thousands of generations of selective breeding and training; they are still wild for all practical purposes. They are just habituated—so accustomed to close contact with humans that they have overcome whatever caution they had through instinct or were taught by their mothers. In some places, habituation is regarded as very dangerous, because it puts wild animals and humans so close together that when someone makes a mistake, there is no margin for error; odds are that some participant is going to get hurt, and if it's a human, then some animal will likely be "removed" in reaction. In other places, such as here at Brooks Falls, the animals are habituated to the apparent advantage of all parties. What price all parties eventually may pay for this advantage remains to be discovered.

The big bear we met at the gate was such an animal; he was a textbook example of habituation. He was so used to having people around, so accustomed to their unthreatening behavior, and so accustomed to not getting food from them that Marsha and I were even less than a threat; we were barely interesting, especially as long as we were on one of the trails on which he was so used to seeing our kind travel. The alarm that Marsha and I had felt was not mutual with him. Though this worked to our advantage that day, habituation is always a restless sort of detente, here at Brooks even more than in your neighbor's backyard.

Every now and then since I started spending time in grizzly bear country, I have had a dream about bears. This isn't something that obsesses me or rules my sleep, and I am only aware of its happening every couple years or so. But the dreams are usually of that most vivid and compelling type that linger like a real memory, especially for the first day after it happens. I can still recite especially exciting moments from several of them.

They are never nightmares. I have yet to be chased by a bear in these dreams, and no blood has ever been shed. But they are always deeply uneasy experiences, without exception characterized by close encounters between me and very large grizzly bears that have complete access to me. They may be wandering around quite calmly in my house while I wait more or less cornered in some room with no doors. The bears aren't intentionally hunting me, but they're almost certain to find me soon. In other dreams, the bears may be as thick as sheep on a hillside while I walk a winding road through the middle of them. Once or twice the landscape has slipped over into a fantastic, Tolkienesque setting of perfectly round trees and rolling hills of storybook tidiness; then the bears were almost cartoonlike, but still as ominous, for all their cuddly caricature.

The horror of actually being mauled is a very hard reality to me, though I'm sure it is largely an intellectual awareness, like my awareness of space flight or playing major league baseball or anything else I have low or no odds of doing. The point is that there seems to be little reason to dwell on the actual experience of that horror, which is probably unimaginable anyway and which written, oral, and even pictorial accounts can only partly portray.

On the other hand, the experience of avoiding bears is something all of us who hike near them know. We know the heightening of attention, the urgent alertness, the looming possibilities. We spend our time, day after day, hopefully waiting for nothing to go wrong. I assume that my dreams are an extension of that exercise, in which I bring the source of the fear out in the open, a lot closer than accustomed. The bears in those dreams don't quite threaten—they never growl or snarl—but they impend so heavily that I am no longer appreciating them as I routinely do when hiking. In the dreams, I am past the stage where I enjoy just being in grizzly country, reveling in the "existence value" of these rare, grand, and hard-to-see creatures. None of that is happening. I never have binoculars or a spotting scope. I am never making notes. I am just waiting, and without exception the bears are there and I have no escape from them if they choose to approach or attack. It isn't the likelihood of attack that makes these dreams so stirring; it is the suspense and the abject vulnerability.

Because of all this, I recognized Brooks. It embodied my dreams. There were large stretches of forest, trail, and riverside where I stood in almost perfect vulnerability. Even the supposed refuges, such as the platforms, with their cute little "no bears" signs, provided no sure sanctuary. The wonderful park service cabin we shared had an enormous kitchen window, a simple set of lightly framed panes that the two biggest bears in Katmai could have stepped through side by side. Along the local trails, there were trees all over the place, some quite climbable, but at any moment when I might look around, few of the trees within range seemed stout enough to withstand one of these big bears if he really wanted to get me out of it. For a week, there was no escape; there was only a scale of insecurity, from the most vulnerable places to those that seemed less worrisome, if only because they were occupied by so many relatively calm, assured people. I never completely escaped the feeling that these people were so calm because they just didn't get it.

We returned to the falls platform after lunch, with no untoward encounters on the way. The bears were taking a break from the falls, but after a while, one, then another, and another came back and resumed their posts, waiting for fish. It was a bright, sunny day, and I had brought my largest lens,

a cheap 100–500mm zoom affair that did a respectable job under such ideal circumstances of abundant, consistent light. Resting my elbows on the platform railing, I banged away for an hour or so, even getting a low-grade but entirely satisfactory version of Mangelsen's immortal image. In mine, the much less enlarged bear was drawing his weight back slightly from the brink of the falls, having just clamped his teeth together on the front end of an airborne salmon. As soon as he had it, he turned and waded to the near shore to eat it. I photographed that—his long, splashy strides and the fish hanging straight and dead from his teeth—until he was out of sight in the trees.

Photography is both an aid and an obstacle. I often wonder how many of the millions of tourists who visit wildlife reserves miss some unforgettable instant because they're too busy fiddling with their gear. I wonder how often I've done that myself. I have friends, passionate photographers, who have intentionally abandoned the art because it got in the way of paying attention; others insist that having a camera in their hands just sharpens their awareness. Being fully present means different things to different people, and we all prefer our own tools to get us there.

I have published only a few dozen pictures, most of them in my own books and magazine articles, and have never pretended that I was in photography for the money. I just love the act of framing a scene, of putting the moment's most powerful image in the right-size little rectangular window of memory, and of capturing some faint essence of what I am seeing now to assist later recollection. It has been worth much more than the cost of all the junky cameras and expensive film and processing over the past thirty years to be able to go back, in some slight way, to so many of the places I've been.

Writer and wilderness advocate T. H. Watkins, who died all too young while I was writing this book, likened our photographic obsession to a modern expression of the ancient urge to hunt. Whether pulling a trigger or triggering a shutter, we let go with the same "Got 'im!" Experience is the trophy, and if we can't hang it on the wall, we can at least drag it out now and then and bore the neighbors. After I started writing, photography became a lazy form of field notes: "I want to remember this setting, but I don't want to stop and write it all down." *Click, click, zoom, click.* But I am always self-conscious about it, aware of a tension between the photographer's urge that inadvertently narrows attention to one part of the scene, and the need to let go of mechanics and just be where I am. In my desire to save it so I can savor it again later, I try never to forget that I'm there right now and should enjoy it firsthand.

Photography, perhaps even more than shopping for curios, exposes the oddness of some of our impulses when we travel. Photographs are badges of success, proof that we got there and did the Right Things. I doubt that I always succeed in containing this impulse, an impulse that I don't think is all bad, but I'm most likely to fail to control it in the presence of the Most Important Right Things. (I took thousands of slides in my two months in Alaska, and when I sorted them, I'm sure I culled and discarded at least half.) Realizing this, at Brooks I figured I would work very hard at first to get some decent contingency photographs, then ease off and carry only my pocket cameras after that, just in case.

At the falls, the professional photographers, often several, occupied the lower, front area of the two levels of the platform. Their heavy tripods, big legs widespread to support massive lenses the size of piano legs, claimed most of the space. Having several friends who are professionals, and admiring their art as I did, I tried very hard not to trip over the tripods or step heavily when any of the photographers were obviously at work. I wondered what could possibly be left to photograph—especially for publication—at this spot after so many years of people with such great equipment standing right here shooting these same bears and salmon in the same poses. But I had to admit that I wouldn't have minded slipping my own camera's body onto one of those mighty lenses for an hour or so.

The national parks in Alaska have an interesting relationship with professional photographers. In good part because the state's congressional delegations are so concerned about encouraging any sort of possible tourist promotion, the parks are strongly advised to give photographers every advantage. When you ride the buses in Denali, you will see virtually no private vehicles along the road, but the few you do see will most likely be those of professional photographers. I once wondered aloud to a park service acquaintance at Denali if I, too, could get a special-use permit to take my own car up that road, so I could exercise my vision as, say, a natural history philosopher, and was told that I might. At Brooks, I was so enthralled by the bears I was seeing that I was slow to realize that the same sort of preferential treatment was occurring right here on the falls platform. Through a kind of unwritten understanding, it seemed that the pros with the big lenses automatically got the front-row positions. Sometimes the entire front row was dominated by their gear. Of course, for all I know, some of them weren't pros at all; they may have been just amateurs like me, but with a lot more money to spend on equipment. The problem, if that's what it was, wasn't one of commerce. It was just a matter of photographic gear dominating the available space.

Assuming our cameras were working (a few weeks earlier, in Denali, both of our only good 35mm cameras had coincidentally suffered mechanical failures in a fifteen-minute period), Marsha and I soon had abundant proof of our visit here. We had reason to hope that we caught a few instants of photogeneity that were special even by the high standards of these bears and their river. As hard as it was to leave, I suggested that it was well past time that I honor another pressing contingency and go fishing.

• • •

Marsha is an artist. She describes herself as "just learning," but she has reached that pleasant stage in learning where even though one may be shy and embarrassed about letting others see one's drawings and paintings, there really is no reason to feel that way. During the few years she has been painting, I have enjoyed her progress with an enthusiasm that surprises me with its intensity. She brings me each new picture and we have long talks about what worked and what didn't, what I recognize and what I don't understand. Because she paints mostly landscapes that we have shared, we get to compare impressions of them. I feel like a minor partner in the creation of fine little worlds, witness to a much stronger magic than photography.

Like me, Marsha was excited about seeing the bears at Brooks. Unlike me, she has no interest in fishing. Her equivalent to my fishing is her art. But we prefer to be together whenever possible, so we sometimes "go fishing" together, which means that she finds a nice spot and sketches while I wander off down the stream. At Brooks, with the relentless warnings about being careful as you travel near the stream, this posed some problems. Though I saw people doing otherwise all week, I was unwilling to go off by myself. The park service recommendation that fishermen should always be accompanied by a "spotter" made perfect sense to me. Over the years that I have been fishing in wild country, I have lost track of the number of times I have fished my way up a stream, completely absorbed in what I was doing, and suddenly looked up to find that I was too close to an elk, a bison, or another hazard. Fishermen, especially those of us who get fairly right-brained about it, are not wholly responsible people. This meant that at Brooks we went fishing almost entirely in the busier areas, where I could count on a variety of people besides me to be watching for bears at least part of the time, and where Marsha could likewise feel a little more free to focus on her art and not need a full-time spotter of her own.

In almost forty years of reading outdoor magazines, I had figured out that the foremost, almost historic, dream of sportfishermen in Alaska was the rainbow trout. When the nineteenth-century fish culturist Seth Green bestowed that magical name on this native western salmonid, he ensured that it would forever hold a place of special affection in the romantic hearts of anglers, and would have an unusual appeal even to the nonangling public. The other most common trout had far less appealing names. What literary or folkloric charm is there in a trout that is "brown," or one that is generically known for the "brook" it lives in? Or consider the other common western trout, the "cutthroat": The name is cruel and off-putting rather than attractive. But the rainbow—here was a label rich in the symbolism of hope and treasure, the very name of beauty.

Anglers and naturalists of course know each of these species and all their subtle genetic variants as animals of unique and laudable qualities, but Green's gift to the rainbow was an example of marketing unmatched in the world of modern sportfishing. Add to that gift the equally seductive modifier "Alaskan," and the combination seems almost overwhelming to the sportsman's ear. I had caught rainbow trout in dozens of rivers but was still susceptible to Green's salesmanship. Alaskan rainbows seemed somehow like the image I had gathered of Alaskan bears: different, wilder, a finer or even higher form of the species.

Brooks Lake is roughly rectangular, about twelve by three miles. Its long axis is oriented toward the east-northeast, and its outlet, where it forms the Brooks River, is on its northernmost corner. From our cabin, it was a short stroll down the shore of the lake to where the river began. We usually had to step over the lines of a few float planes tied to shore; evidently, landings were easier here than at Naknek Lake, where it got rough in high winds.

I love rivers from end to end, but I am most enchanted by their genesis. Whether they emerge from a mountainside seep, gush from some valley-bottom spring, or just leak out from under a snowbank, their beginning appeals to me beyond all reason. Every time I see such a beginning, I have to stop and stare at it, and if anyone is with me, they must endure my little sermon: Right here, with no fanfare and very little notice even among my fellow anglers, something starts that will carry great changes across the landscape, that will define its ecology and will likewise shape its human society. The traditional celebration of the river as a flowing process tends to focus on its gathering of power, commerce, and history as it rolls toward its goal, and the river's poetic potential is most heavily exploited as it approaches the sea. But there seems so much more promise, so much more to celebrate back at the headwaters, where the whole saga still lies ahead and the river's fortunes are still up for grabs.

But Brooks River is not like most of my familiar mountain streams, which do indeed begin from seeps and snowbanks and only mature and broaden with time and miles and the contribution of many other streams. Brooks is born adult, full-size the instant the lake's surface meets a long ledge of rock and bends a couple degrees down and over, accelerating from the imperceptible rate of flow that characterizes most lakes to the riffled surface of a running river.

Nonfishermen, looking at the first straight stretch of this river as it leaves the lake and before it makes a smart right turn to begin its crossing of the isthmus, would see it as little different from the lake it just left. To them it would seem just another undifferentiated flat surface of water. But to the practiced eye, it is a wonderland of distinct and describable places—quieter reaches, deep runs, graveled shallows, a hundred little nooks and corners—all signaled or at least suggested by that surface, which upon closer examination is anything but flat. Its topography, though fluid, reveals patterns: slower rippled stretches that suggest greater depth; long, narrow slicks behind slightly submerged boulders; bright, wide shallows where finer particles have accumulated to build up quiet shoals. Friends of mine have written entire books about the craft of "reading" a trout stream; it is a fine skill, a way to open windows on hidden treasures. Whether practiced by a fisherman with specific interests or a naturalist in a more expansive mood, such topographic interpretation suggests which types of life inhabit each place, and even from the shore, I could see a number of places in this first stretch of the Brooks River that announced trout as plainly as neon signs.

I had put on my waders and vest back at the cabin. While Marsha sought a good place to settle, I waded out to the closest of these aquatic invitations, a deeper run only a few yards downstream from the "edge" of the lake. I was standing up to my thighs in the river, and the run, which was only about twenty feet from me, was considerably deeper. For the first few casts, I drifted a small elk-hair caddis, a miraculously buoyant and visible fly, over the riffle because Tom Ferguson had told me to start with one just in case the rainbows were looking up right then and would feed on the surface. There was no response, so I switched to a pheasant-tail nymph, so named because its body was made almost entirely of the auburn-colored barbules of a pheasant's tail feathers, which for some reason of texture and shade and natural indistinctiveness of outline have a singular effect on the feeding urge of trout.

The response to this fly was dramatic. I cast it up to the edge of the lake, several feet upstream of the actual run, so that it would have time to sink before getting to what I imagined to be the "best" water. About the time it reached that water, it was wrenched from its course with the power only a big fish could exercise. As I lifted the rod tip to tighten the line, a rainbow trout of just over twenty inches emerged from the river in a perfect imitation of the towering leaps so popular in mid-twentieth-century sporting art, which portrayed the fish as a kind of silver missile shedding water as it climbed into the sky. Before me and on down the stream to my right, this trout leaped several times, shedding artistic clichés and river water in random, sparkling mists. As excited as I was, I still had time to reflect hastily on the sudden *realness* of another part of Alaska, and to laugh.

One controls a large fish like this, especially when playing it in fast water on a fairly light leader, by stages. At first, the fish's runs and leaps are too strong to do more than tolerate, yielding line from the reel—which chatters most satisfactorily when the fish tears across the river, a noise the more hyperbolic fishing writers describe as "screaming"—dropping the rod tip when the fish leaps, so that the line is slack and less likely to be broken by the greater twisting quickness of the air-free fish (this is nicely called "bowing to the fish," and often the jumps happen too fast for you to do any such thing), and hoping mostly to tire it out a little. Though for many years anglers sought to get as many jumps and runs from a fish as possible—a measure of the success of the sport—the modern sensibility aims for the quickest possible landing, to leave the fish enough energy so that it is not too exhausted to recover. After a minute or two, and two or three jumps, it is possible to retrieve line against the swimming fish, getting it closer, working it toward shore. Often, while these first minutes are passing, it is wise to move downstream, and if the fish chooses to go there, as mine did, it is necessary to follow. I chased it in that undignified, splashy way that knee-deep, rocky-bottomed rivers require, gaining and giving back line as the fish sought various refuges along the way and then broke into the open again with a surge of flight.

I finally beached the fish on a shallow bar of small, dark rocks and gravel just upstream from the river's first turn.

Marsha's photographs of this first encounter with the local rainbows show me sloshing away from the camera, sometimes partly obscured by the hanging foliage along the shore; then me farther away, my rod bent in a low, flat arc, with the white line stretched taut across the current and pinpointing an invisible fish in deeper water; then me kneeling over the fish on the gravel bar, hurriedly taking a photograph of it before holding it upright in a slow current to revive it.

If you don't fish, this whole process may seem as pointless as golf or bridge seems to me. If you do fish, you will know the exhilaration of this contact with something wild, fragile, and so barely managed even when it is in one's own hands. In a way, it's rather like baseball, with stretches of what would appear to the casual observer to be inactivity, alternated with frenetic action, further alternated with moments of reflection and even wonder. In another way, it's a variation on the "Got 'im!" by which we make some small claim on an admired thing that even as we hold it stays somehow beyond our reach. I repeated parts of this exercise seven times in an hour, finally landing three of the fish. One other as big as any of them made two consecutive Polaris-style launches almost head-high as soon as it felt the hook, throwing the fly at the top of the second jump. Perhaps the most exciting thing for me right then was that Marsha got to see it all. I even hurried one of the fish to her for a look at it up close before I let it go.

"Rainbow trout" is a misnomer. There isn't actually a whole rainbow of colors on the side. Like many creatures, the rainbow trout features the countershading so common as an aid to concealing coloration, with its underside lighter than its back. But the rainbow trout adds an almost lurid flourish: a crimson band that runs the length of its side, clear from the gill plate to the tail. This one broad band of red provides the only bright color, but it is complemented with the pale creamy shades of the belly and the darker silver-gray or blue-gray shades of the back, so that the visual effect is of a progression of shades, lighter to darker from belly to back, with red in the middle. The visual effect is also of a luminosity that in some specimens, including mine that day, seems stronger than mere reflected light could generate. It is also a life effect, for within moments after death, all the shades grow dull and sad.

Because I find it somewhat obscure—and therefore presume you won't be interested—I am glossing over a debate among taxonomists, whose very job is sorting out the obscure, about the rainbow. It is maintained by some that there is another fish in many parts of the West that should be called not a rainbow, but a redband. I suspect that this is true, but for now I side with all the casual observers to whom all these fish are rainbows that just display different tendencies toward having or lacking the red band. Coastal fish like the ones I caught are regarded by the more critical observers as being the least colorful. None of the fish I caught had the red stripe; they sported the shades I would normally associate with freshly arrived salmon or seagoing rainbows, which enter the rivers in an almost metallic two-tone—silver on the sides and gun-metal blue-gray on the back. I wondered, briefly, if perhaps these rainbows moved down to the sea, but studies in the 1980s, in which radio transmitters were implanted in a few dozen local rainbow trout, revealed that though the fish do wander in and out of the river to Naknek and Brooks lakes, they don't seem to go any farther than that.

As for their size, I had already picked up enough local lore to know that these were not exceptional fish for the area. Wherever I go, I catch average fish at best. Biologists could save great quantities of money spent on population surveys by having me fish their water for a few days; what I land will represent the typical fish in the population, and biologists can be especially confident in announcing that the trophy fish in the population are between fifty and one hundred percent longer than the length of my biggest fish. And this was Alaska, after all. Enormous schools of thirty-inch rainbows swim through the pages of books and articles on Alaska fishing. The lodge had pictures of such monsters, many taken from boats in the lake. From my recently acquired local informants, some of whom I already trusted completely, I heard of catches of rainbows up to twenty-seven inches in the river itself. This was all interesting, but I didn't have room for a lot of disappointment in my heart right then; these fish were everything I could have hoped for.

One evening in Anchorage, after we returned from Katmai, Marsha took me along to a nice dinner that she needed to attend for work reasons. There were a number of park service people there, as well as some other friends. Over dinner, Bill Pierce, who now knew of my enthusiasm for fish and fishing, asked me if I also planned to do some halibut fishing while I was in Alaska. The halibut fishing was pretty good right then, and the charter boats were very busy.

I happened to be eating halibut as we spoke. It is my favorite eating fish, and one of the few ocean species that my reading suggests to me it is still possible to eat with little guilt of participating in an extinction event, because at least along the Pacific coast the harvest is well managed. But I answered Bill by saying that the idea of spending a day in a little boat rocking around on the open ocean, puking my guts out at regular intervals, for the chance to winch an animal the size of a German shepherd up through three hundred feet of cold seawater just didn't appeal to me. Bill smiled his big, generous smile and suggested that he knew what I meant, but that I might be surprised if I tried it.

He might have been right about that. We agreed that after it was over I would, after all, have a chunk of fresh halibut the size of a German shepherd. This didn't persuade me, though, because we were getting equally fresh halibut from the local store and bypassing the part about the boat. But it did remind me for the thousandth time how marvelous and vexing an institution sportfishing is.

After my first six summers fly-fishing in Yellowstone, I spent five years, 1977 to 1982, as executive director of the American Museum of Fly Fishing in Vermont. Here I became immersed in what, over the course of several centuries, had become a genuine subculture within the society of anglers. No type of fisherman, whether cane-pole novice, deep-sea big-game hunter, or high-tech bass boater, is without foibles or hilarious stereotype. I don't mean to suggest that fly fishermen are special; they suggest that themselves often enough. What I mean to say is that among all anglers, we fly fishers have taken divergent social evolution about as far as it can go without serious harm to the greater society we inhabit. Of all kinds of fishermen, we may have spent the most time on our self-consciousness-building exercises, and have put the most effort into perceiving ourselves as different from all the rest.

What Brooks reminded me of was that for all this effort at distinguishing ourselves from other fishermen, we fly fishers have retained all the internal divisiveness and wacky individual opinions that human nature could generate. In only a few days, and in conversations with only a few locals, I identified at least four different sets of fly fishers at Brooks River.

There were the hard-core rainbow trout devotees, to whom the salmon might as well have been carp. One of these men announced with near indignation, when I told him that the salmon run wasn't amounting to much yet, "I'm not here for the reds—I'm here for the rainbows!" (Red is a nickname for the sockeye salmon.) Apparently quite a few of these rainbow fishermen come to Brooks when the salmon aren't running, to avoid the crowds of salmon and salmon fishermen. Historian Frank Norris, who has spent years studying the documentary record of Katmai, tells me that anglers at Brooks were like this in the 1950s, when salmon were perceived as a commercial fish and rainbows as a sport fish.

There were the people I thought of as salmon duffers, casual tourist fishermen who may have done little or no fly-fishing but were game to try. Patient guides from one of the lodges in the region would appear with three or four of these men in a little knot behind them, herd them into position in a likely stretch of river, give them the basics of repeatedly winging a heavily weighted fly into the deep water, and wait for someone to have a hookup. Whether the fish actually tried to eat the fly or just got snagged in a fin, there was plenty of action to keep the duffers happy. They were for the most part cheerful guys, easy to talk to.

There were the serious salmon fishermen. I saw only a few of these, but they were deadly effective, and may have been the hardest-concentrating group of all. They often had a deep experience of the sport, and usually had at least one unique perspective on how best to catch the fish. A young, dark-haired man named Jake, who worked at the lodge, was the best I saw. He had an extraordinary ability to see the fish at great distances and to tell, when the rest of us could see nothing but vague shapes in the shiny water, when a fish had shown interest in the fly as it went past. With every cast, he conducted a quiet, almost inaudible personal monologue with himself, a continuous discussion of the progress of the fly and the locations of the fish, all of which he could see much better than the rest of us could. (For all I know, he was also talking to the fish; I often do.) He fair-hooked three or four times as many fish as anybody else, with no fanfare. He also had a generosity of spirit that was heartwarming, sharing split shot when I ran low and yielding his spot to another fisherman who wasn't getting any hits, all in keeping with the Waltonian ideal that I have encountered a surprising number of times as a stranger on many North American streams.

And there were people like me, who were so excited to be in Alaska, casting over anything that lived in this river, that they hurried from one possibility to the next, hardly able to relax fully into any one sporting opportunity because so many others were beckoning. Looking back on my week at Brooks, I am most often haunted by the image of small, quiet rises of fish in the middle of deeper pools of the river and along the shore of Brooks Lake. A mere round ruffling of the surface, a ring only a few inches across, these little riseforms were caused by arctic grayling, an enchanting fish. But I never could tear myself away from the salmon and rainbows long enough to go after them. Hog Heaven is not necessarily a place of great contentment, or of simple satisfactions.

After dinner I wanted to fish for salmon, and the practical place to do that was near the pontoon bridge, where there were usually other fishermen. Most of the time during the busier part of the day, the park service stationed a ranger, an experienced volunteer, or some other staff member on the platform at the bridge just as they did at the falls. They were kept busy monitoring traffic to the falls and conferring with other staff people at the falls, the lodge, and anywhere else a bear might be, but they had time to keep an eye on the lowest bends of the river, where fishermen were often too preoccupied and low to the water to see a bear approaching through the high grass and mixed forest that line the stream. For Marsha's purposes, the possibilities of bear watching or painting or just sitting and enjoying Alaska were about as good at the mouth of the river as at the falls, so while I fished, she stayed near the platform by the bridge.

Downstream of the bridge, the river widened into a near bay. There were a few grassy islands right where the river joined Naknek Lake. Though very little of the water was over a fisherman's head, most of us concentrated in a few places, the most popular being the south shore of the river right downstream of the bridge. Here, four or five fishermen had lined up along the shore or in the shallows, making a row of fishermen about fifteen feet apart. They made short casts out into the deeper water in front of them, and once in a while someone would hook a fish. From the platform behind them or the bridge just upstream of them, I could look down into the water and see a dark, irregular blob moving restlessly in the slow current. This was a school of two or three dozen sockeye salmon, fresh in from their trip out of Bristol Bay, up the Naknek River, across Naknek Lake, and into Brooks River.

Conventional wisdom has it that salmon, especially those newly returned from the open ocean, don't like going under bridges. The pontoon bridge was only a foot or so off the water and made a dark shadow. I had the impression that each new pod of fish grouped in this spot until one of them made the first move to pass under the very low pontoon bridge; this would suggest that they didn't like that bridge shadow.

But I also had the impression that this stretch of water below the bridge was much like several other resting places where the salmon concentrated upstream of the bridge; maybe the salmon stopped there for other reasons. The salmon's mind is inaccessible to me in this and many other questions, the most pressing of which right then was how to catch it.

All the species of Pacific salmon are anadromous, terminally so. Anadromy is the act of being hatched in fresh water, migrating to salt water while still small and growing large there, then returning to the very same fresh water—to the very same reach of the very same river—to spawn and die. Some other species that make this same trip, such as Pacific coast steelhead (a sea-run form of the rainbow trout) and Atlantic salmon, don't die. They are physiologically able to make the trip again and again, as long as their health and predators allow them to, though few manage it more than twice. But all Pacific salmon, including these sockeyes we were fishing for, will die upon completion of the spawning run. Here at Brooks, their living but failing bodies, like discarded padded envelopes after the most important contents have been delivered, will drift back downstream and cause a second feeding sensation among the bears in the early fall.

Anadromy is for me one of the great wonders of the natural world, and it provides me with a great and sentimental attachment to this kind of fishing. I fish for salmon and steelhead with a feeling of participation in the closing moments of a great odyssey. They have wandered far and unknown courses in the deep Pacific, feeding and growing for years before turning for home to close the epic circle of their lives. (A British friend calls them "silver tourists.") They have spent thousands of generations developing the biochemical flexibility, strength, and numbers required to take not only the hardships, but also the inevitable losses needed to turn such prodigious journeying into a successful survival strategy. It is hard to imagine evidence of a more determined spirit—if not in the individual fish, then in the population to which they contribute their small individuality. They make the arctic tern's longer but much quicker migration look almost easy.

They do all that, and then, just as they reach their front door, they find all of us in their way. Like so many others that welcome them home—eagles, otters, seals, bears, and a hundred smaller life forms that benefit from some stage of their return, death, and decay—I may not seem the most salutary of greeters from the salmon's point of view, but from my point of view, rarely is fishing more purely a form of celebration of the valor of wildlife than when I can cast over water connected to the sea and running with these long-awaited travelers.

But fishing for salmon is remarkably different from almost every other form of sportfishing, because the salmon don't eat. Once their metabolisms have undergone the biochemical adjustment to fresh water, their energies are aimed solely at successfully completing the trip and spawning. Procreation is their only pursuit, and their entire digestive tracts might as well atrophy and vanish. Even the Atlantic salmon and steelhead, species that might survive spawning and return to the ocean, rarely eat. I know of exceptions, but for practical purposes—those being the purposes of an eager angler looking over a group of freshly arrived wild salmon—the exceptions are so rare that they just reinforce the rule.

Fishing is all about getting the fish to eat something that has a hook in it. If the fish is not eating in the first place, that is naturally much harder to achieve. For the past couple centuries, it has been common knowledge among most sportfishermen on the Pacific coast that their salmon would not take a fly, but for much of that time, a few anglers were figuring out how to make them do just that.

"Fly" is perhaps the foremost puzzling term in the sport of fly-fishing. As fly-fishing existed several hundred years ago in Europe and England, its practitioners tied various combinations of fur and feathers onto small hooks to imitate a variety of insects. Since then, the term has stuck, though the sport has broadened its life imitations to include everything from minnows to baby muskrats to crayfish. Though they don't imitate real-life insects, these things are still called flies. People fly-fish with them for bluegills, trout, barracuda, and other fish, all the way up to sailfish and tarpon the size of kayaks.

Alaskan anglers have contributed to this diversification of fly types with some innovations of their own. Noticing that some species of sport fish, such as the Dolly Varden char, follow salmon migrations to feast on the sloughing flesh of the decaying carcasses, Alaskans have developed a "flesh fly," which in shade and contour is a perfect imitation of a small chunk of loose salmon meat.

Debates rage on the "appropriateness" or "sportsmanship" of many practices in the sport. Some abhor the use of any added weight on the line or fly. Others prefer only flies that float on the surface of the water, and some privately owned British streams allow no other kind of flies. Through these debates, fishing regulations are framed and reframed, and general practice out there on the river evolves, but in most American fishing contexts, at least, there is huge room for practicing the sport however you prefer, and for feeling however you choose to feel about the preferences of your fellow anglers. This area of personal preference is fly-fishing's nearest equivalent to the passions displayed by Red Sox,

Yankee, and Tiger fans; such choices are not susceptible to simple, objective analysis, and that may be what makes them so durable and important to the sport's vitality.

In the Old World, Atlantic salmon have been caught on flies for centuries, but in the past two hundred years, the salmon fly has become a separate folk art. No one knew for sure why a salmon might suddenly strike a given fly, because its decision was not tied directly to its need for food. This uncertainty opened up a terrific hole in the aesthetic fabric of the sport, one that we have been filling ever since with our wildest imaginings. Freed from the necessity of imitating any specific life form or type of food, and likewise freed from any real understanding of what the salmon was up to when it did strike, craftsmen developed hundreds of elegant, complex flies that looked like nothing at all. As the British Empire's global trade network made available to fly tiers nature's most bizarre and exotic materials—iridescent tropical feathers, strangely hued monkey skins, polar bear hair of the softest translucency, and hundreds of other rare visual marvels—the salmon fly passed into its own little aesthetic universe, a kind of post-modern baroque abstract impressionism. The idea of the fly as an imitation of life was supplanted by an idea of the fly as independent of life, and the result was a beautiful thing that made no sense but its own and obeyed only its makers' unique aesthetic rather than any biology-based empiricism.

More recently, Pacific salmon fly fishers have followed a similar theme but in very different directions. Leaning heavily on fluorescent dyes, they have created an ungodly kaleidoscopic welter of patterns. Flies for the largest species, king salmon that run to sixty pounds and more, look like moldy radioactive golf balls trailing Christmas tree tinsel and angel's hair. Some patterns are rough neon outlines of small fish, expressing the hope that even though the salmon may no longer feed, they might have pleasant memories of doing so and strike from some conditioned response, or just from nostalgia—who knows? Other patterns lean heavily to fleshy pinks, the gaudier the better, in hopes that they might trigger some memory of protein-rich shrimp. Mixed in are even some obvious imitations of river life, such as large stonefly nymphs; no harm in hedging your bet on the chance that you might fish over a salmon that in some tangled piscine synapses still reacts to the aquatic insects of her parrhood days. Choosing a fly for these fish is the sport's greatest crap shoot, and it inspires a gambler's reckless confidence.

Bill Pierce and other people told me that Bill Allan was the resident expert on the local fishing. Allan and his wife, Pat, are park service volunteers who have spent many summers at Brooks. They put in many patient, cheerful hours at the platforms, staffing the visitor center, and otherwise helping visitors, and in exchange they earn the right to live here all summer. Bill, with whom I checked in daily as much for moral support as for actual advice ("Keep casting; you'll catch them"), gave me a few flies of a flaming lime color with bead-chain eyes at the heads. He said they were what was working that week, so I stuck with them and caught some fish.

That first evening fishing for the sockeyes, in an act of gracious cordiality for someone whose name I did not even know yet, young Jake invited me to wade into the first position, just a few feet downstream of the bridge. The most important trick that a century of experimentation has come up with for getting most Pacific salmon to take a fly was making it easy for them to do so, which meant getting the fly right down in front of their faces and drifting it past them again and again. This was achieved through weighting the fly itself with metal (thus the bead-chain eyes) and biting a few small lead split shot in a row onto the leader. This done, I lobbed the awkward arrangement upstream of the salmon blob. Every few casts there at first, I'd hang the whole rattling affair up on the bridge's railing. Then I let it sink, and felt it bump along the bottom and through the school of fish. The slightest hesitation or tug, suggestive of contact with a fish, triggered my strike. More often than not, the fish would just be snagged—my fly had hung up momentarily on its fin or back, and it hadn't intended to take.

I hooked and lost one in a few seconds' time, then a few minutes later hooked another firmly. As I set the hook, the fish left the group in front of me and headed down the river, as if planning to revisit the lake or return to Bristol Bay. As I followed it toward the lake, the other fishermen stepped back or reeled in to let me through. Though it had reacted to being hooked with less initial excitement than had the rainbows at the other end of the river, the salmon ran with just as much speed. I could judge this from the pitch of the reel's "screaming" drag as the line went out. It jumped just as powerfully, too, and more impressively.

There is a size, somewhere around eighteen inches, past which all jumping fish look gigantic in the air. This sockeye, at two feet long and perhaps six pounds (an average fish, of course), looked like a silver whale, and it came back into the water with a ponderous smack that made me fear for the well-being of the leader and the hold of the fly.

In setting the hook, there is a satisfaction similar to that in Isak Dinesen's description of shooting a lion:

> I stood, panting, in the grass, aglow with the plentipotence that a shot gives you, because you take effect at a distance.

But as the fish recedes from reach, the distance becomes too great, and I feel more like a witness than a participant. When the action is taking place so much farther from me, a hundred feet or more, my effect seems perilously attenuated, and a helplessness sets in, to the near exclusion of the authority I thought I was exercising when I first set the hook.

Everything held just fine, though, and after a few minutes of reeling and yielding and reeling some more, I had the fish close enough that I could back away from the water and slide it onto the grass. Bill's little, green, bug-eyed monstrosity was firmly hooked in the hinge of the jaw. I removed it, held the fish up for a quick photograph by Marsha, and eased it back into the water. It swam away to resume its upstream course, where it would soon face a more determined predator at the falls.

Not Visitor-Friendly

But when Alaska wants something, every son of a bitch out there thinks he owns Alaska and you can't get anything done!
—Alaska governor Wally Hickel, 1992

In early June, toward the end of our long drive from Montana, Henry and I entered Alaska by way of the Top-of-the-World Highway, a seasonal gravel road that runs from the Yukon River ferry at Dawson City, in Canada's Yukon Territory, across the border into Alaska. From there we made our way to Fairbanks, taking a few side roads and stopping in small communities and wide spots along the way, to buy gas or food, or just to learn about the place.

The first person with whom we spoke at any length was a white, middle-aged man in jeans and a flannel shirt, and we were not prepared. At least I wasn't. Later, Henry and I talked it over and decided we needed a plan: The next time we had to talk to somebody in roadside Alaska, and perhaps even in towns, we would introduce ourselves as high school teachers off on a summer lark in the Far North. Anything was better than telling people that we worked for the federal government. This wasn't so much because we were afraid of outright violence—though I gathered such fear was justified some-times—as it was a matter of not wanting to waste time on the hassle and annoyance of uninvited lectures and rants.

Americans are fond of griping about their government—I certainly seem to be. But Americans who do not live in the West or the Far North generally have no idea of the appalling hostility federal employees face in those places. In the minds and hearts of many of the West's federal employees, especially those who work in field units of the large land-management agencies responsible for caring for so much western terrain, the bombing of the federal building in Oklahoma City may have been a horrific tragedy, but it could not have been a sur-prise. Land-management agency staffs are routinely subjected to harassment bordering on terrorism, and even when things are relatively calm, the newspapers run citizens' rage-filled letters about the awful feds. This is more than a tradition; it is part of western culture. In *Searching for Yellowstone* (1997), I pointed out that most American citizens would be amazed at the extent to which even Yellowstone National Park, a great icon and symbol of so many pleasant and affirmative things in our society, is viewed as a force for evil in the surrounding region. The park ranger, for most Americans the personifica-tion of Smokey Bear's wholesome values—of good in the wilderness—is for many local people the bad guy.

But even at that, ranger friends who had worked in Alaska over the years told me that I hadn't seen anything yet; that for unadulterated outrage, I needed to talk to some Alaskans. This first one proved them right. In seeming friendliness, he opened the conversation the way many of us do when meet-ing a stranger—he asked me where I was from. Because of all the horror stories I'd heard, I was nervous, but I told him: Wyoming. He then asked the question that I later realized was the only one he really wanted to ask: What do you do there? I told him I worked for the National Park Service (this, oddly enough, seemed less dangerous than telling him I was a writer)—and at that moment, the conversation, at least in any orthodox definition of the term, ceased. He immediately launched into a tirade about the evils of the park service.

Actually, it was remarkable, a study in the power of self-serving opinion over reality. I would not be surprised to learn that there are many people in these little towns who can make well-reasoned criticisms of current federal stewardship of Alaska's public lands, but I had not just met one of them. On the other hand, his presentation had an oddly compelling quality. Vastly misinformed about forestry, wildlife, and the nature of federal governance, he was still well spoken. His grammar, even under the formidable pressure of his indignation, remained perfect. And he seemed like a nice enough guy, otherwise.

The park service, he said, was ruining everything. People couldn't do what they had always done anymore. The park service wouldn't let him shoot wolves from airplanes. With rangers out there patrolling and using radios, and those cameras they have mounted out there taking a picture every four seconds, it's not a wilderness anymore. This inventory of lost freedoms went on for a minute or two, internal contradictions piling up on each other (radios and cameras compromised the wilderness, but shooting wolves from airplanes did not?) in an avalanche of pet peeves. I did attempt a couple conciliatory remarks about how there were other people with different viewpoints, and he guessed there must be, but he obviously thought they were fools.

This was happening along the side of the main road, where we had stopped for a moment. Henry was still in the car, but as the tirade rolled on, he got out and walked around to the driver's side, where I stood listening to the man. I was surprised to find out how edgy I was. Henry or I (it might have been me, in a weak-willed attempt to deflect some of the man's attention) admitted that Henry worked for the forest service, which set off another tirade.

Henry is in very good shape. He takes care of himself and had lately taken up the study of certain martial arts with the same intense focus he applies to everything he does. During our trip up through the Yukon, whenever I hiked off to fish some promising stream, he stayed by the car and ran through his moves (with or without his rubber training knife), which I rather disrespectfully referred to as "doing his thousand deaths." So when the man gave Henry a challenging look and asked, in what I later learned was a widespread rhetorical distinction, "Are you a tree *cutter* or a tree *saver?*" and I saw a hard glint come into Henry's eyes, I began to worry about where this was heading.

"I'm a tree saver," Henry said proudly, even defiantly, to the man, who to my relief took it with the same lack of interest that he had shown in my less assertive responses. This really wasn't a conversation. It was just a series of opportunities for the man to explore new avenues of disapproval. Mention of the forest service reminded him that a friend of his—that most authoritative of conversational citations—had told him that ten years was a good cycle for harvesting hardwood forests, because all those clear-cuts made for really big deer populations. And on and on.

It took us a few minutes to extricate ourselves, which we did politely. The man never stopped being civil. It was almost as if he didn't think we should take all these criticisms personally. But we took the whole thing very hard. Both of us had some reason to regard ourselves as dedicated professional conservationists and hard-working public servants, and this sort of uninformed verbal assault, even if it was a fact of life in our lower-forty-eight jobs, was just too much. We hadn't come all this way to such an exciting and beautiful place just to listen to such idiotic crap.

This was a town we had some interest in, though I can't recall why. But as soon as we escaped, we discovered that we both wanted to leave as fast as we could. We went into a nearby store for some junk food and then were on our way. It was late in the day and time to be setting up camp. But we had to go, and we were confident that at least some of the local Alaskans wouldn't mind.

We spent the first hour of the drive sputtering about the man's ill-considered lecture. I wondered if the remarks about the cameras were like the "black helicopter" rhetoric so common in the rural West, where too many people flatter themselves that the federal government cares enough to spend enormous amounts of money watching their little doings with high-tech surveillance equipment. (These are perhaps the same people who call Marsha at her park service office to ask her if the rumors are true that ten thousand United Nations troops are secretly training in the backcountry of Yellowstone National Park.) Henry doubted this; he thought that the man was probably just referring to standard wildlife censusing cameras that biologists use in many places, and that his objection to the cameras was the introduction of such technology into the wilderness. I could sympathize with anyone who regarded such equipment as unattractive in wild country, but again ran up against the man's conviction that shooting wolves from airplanes was somehow not a greater intrusion. We could hardly imagine what to make of his baffling misunderstanding of logging cycles in hardwood forests, but he clearly had the embarrassingly old-fashioned sportsman's certainty that really high deer populations were worth any price the forest might pay in the loss of habitat for other species.

But I kept coming back to the shooting-wolves-from-airplanes complaint. In the lower forty-eight for many years, the fight against this Alaskan practice had become a great public cause, and the practice of killing wolves that way was so universally regarded as barbaric that it was kind of exciting to meet an actual practitioner. It wasn't that I objected in principal to predator control, which I knew had arguable biological rationales behind it in some circumstances. It was that I was hearing an actual hard-liner on the subject. The real Alaska was indeed a wonderful place.

Katmai National Monument was created in 1918, long before the spate of legislation that created all the newer Alaskan parks. Among Alaska's national park sites, only a small historic site at Sitka, set aside in 1910, and Denali itself, established as Mount McKinley National Park in 1917, are older. Katmai underwent a series of controversial enlargements before becoming a national park and preserve in 1980, as part of the Alaska Lands Act.

Two things characterized the monument's early years. The first was the consistent lack of attention paid to it by the National Park Service. The park service was almost criminally underfunded and understaffed in Alaska back then, but still it is amazing that no park service employee even visited Katmai for nineteen years, when Mount McKinley's chief ranger spent a single day there. Agency administrators took more than thirty years to issue the first regulations for the monument, which was generating very little public interest and even less visitation by anyone even vaguely resembling tourists. Locals trapped, hunted, and prospected at will, but, though I despise this kind of abuse of public lands, I have to admit that these people probably did little permanent harm, if they even did much temporary harm.

Representatives of other institutions, and of federal and territorial agencies, occasionally visited Katmai. Depending upon their specialty, they tried to do some helpful law enforcement, studied local conditions, and had their way with the place as they saw fit. In 1920, for example, the U.S. Bureau of Fisheries began operations at Brooks. Believing that the fish could use some help in getting over the falls, they dynamited the stone on the north side of the river at the falls, hoping to ease the salmon's trip up the river; it isn't clear how much this helped the fish. Then, at midcentury, the bureau built an actual fish ladder on the south shore. Reflecting their era's most common, husbandry-oriented attitudes toward fisheries resources, these people saw nature as something that could be improved on, even in a supposedly wild setting. The ladder, though blocked at the upper end in 1973 by the park service, still exists, and I imagine that only a few visitors notice it right there next to the falls viewing platform; I only noticed that there was some odd-looking overgrown stonework there. To the extent that management occurred, it was haphazard, occasional, and, like the poaching, probably not all that harmful.

The other distinctive characteristic of Katmai's early years was the Territory of Alaska's resistance to its very existence. This resistance, though fueled by the federal government's exasperating unwillingness to do anything with the monument, was mostly the result of Alaskan disapproval of any such withholding of potential resources from the use of local interests. Again and again, recommendations were offered by territorial politicians and local citizens' groups that the monument be abolished. Those people who recognized that complete abolition of the monument was unlikely made many other specific suggestions, all aimed at improving the access of commerce to the area. They proposed to open it to mineral development, commercial fishing and clamming (with attendant canneries), trapping, and other activities that park service leaders regarded as beyond the scope of the monument's appropriate uses. Most of these proposals were fought off, and the monument survived and grew.

After 1950 or so, when Katmai first got a regular park service staff person on site, park service inattention gradually subsided, as did Alaskan determination to abolish the monument. Slowly the staff increased. More studies were conducted of ecological matters and pressing management issues. Visitors trickled in, then began to flow, which meant that commerce likewise began to flow. Many plans for developments were made and debated, a few lodges appeared, and Brooks became the only major developed public attraction, with comfortable concessioner services and a reasonable amount of attention from park service rangers. (There are other more remote lodges in Katmai.) As with all such large areas of public land, every step in this process and every change in administration has been accompanied by controversy and emotional debate. Frank Norris's 539-page *Isolated Paradise: An Administrative History of the Katmai and Aniakchak National Park Units* (1996) is an outstanding scholarly monument to this painful, stumbling process.

About 227 million of Alaska's 365 million acres of land are managed by federal agencies. This does not make Alaska unique; equal or larger percentages of Utah, Nevada (the champion, at almost eighty-three percent), and Idaho are similarly managed, as are at least a third of the lands in six other western states. What makes Alaska unusual is that almost all of its non-federal lands are managed by other agencies. Native corporations and the state own most of the rest. One percent of Alaska is in private hands, and only about one-twentieth of that is in any way developed. There are great and bitter disagreements over the justice of these proportions, which lie behind every land issue reported in many books and articles about Alaska.

To many Alaskans, few things are more unfair than setting aside so much of the state in parks and reserves where their activities are restricted. Alaskans are certainly entitled to this opinion, but what I have always found most interesting about it is the myopic definition it gives the public domain. To these people, the park service is an intruder here. To me, and apparently to a great many other members of the public who share ownership of this domain, the park service is just the manager of our common lands. Three hundred million or so non-Alaskans and Alaskans are equally entitled to a voice in deciding how those lands should be managed. That first Alaskan that Henry and I met (and Governor Hickel, quoted at the beginning of this chapter) talked as if all these lands were his personal backyard, and for a long time that was exactly how Alaskans were free to act. If I were them, I'd resent the change too. On my more cynical days, I recognized myself as this man's worst nightmare: an outsider who not only knew that this land was mine, but who also cared how it should be managed. To him the park service was Big Brother, interfering with his freedom. To me, the park service was just an instrument of the public will. Like any federal bureaucracy, its performance may rarely live up to the public's ideals and dreams, but demonizing an agency as an evil force is a convenient way of sidestepping the harder realities.

Neither the local nor the national interests have positions that are uniformly held by all parties. Alaskans are no more of a mind than are other Americans. No one can convincingly claim (except to oneself) to love the land more than anybody else does, or to have its best interests more at heart. Even if one could, the intensity of one's affection for a place is no proof of good judgment about how it should be managed. Neither is how long one has lived there.

Where these public-land debates typically leave us is in stalemates that are broken only if all parties give in a little and settle for less than they wanted but more than their opponents wanted them to have. But that seems less and less satisfying to me. Indeed, I have often thought that rather than put every piece of public land through the compromise mill that ends up not fully satisfying anybody, it might be better for somebody to just surrender entirely.

For example, what if my preference for some big chunk of land might be absolutely no development? If I'm that much of a purist, then the land is more or less ruined if it even gets a modest amount of development. If I can't have my preference, might it be better just to let our indignant Alaskan do his best according to his own lights, however dim I might think they are? At least something would be gotten right then—at least one preference and one dream would be fully honored. At least some version of Alaska could remain especially real.

Of course, it doesn't work that way. Not only do I not want to give up, and have no way of knowing for sure when I have lost, but neither does anybody else. I was often reminded of this dilemma at Brooks. At first glance, even with its turmoil of interacting bears and people, Brooks seems almost idyllic in its devotion to the simple mission of caring for nature so that people can most fully enjoy it. But it spends its full share of time in the insider-outsider vise, and the turmoil is the most urgent proof of the pressure. It is a turmoil heightened by the growing interest in visiting the place and enjoying its bears, its fish, and its mood.

•   •   •

The marvelous concentrations of bears at Brooks River are not known to be a long-term phenomenon in the twentieth century. For reasons that are not well understood, the bears have been changing the timing of their use of the salmon run, and there are more bears involved than there used to be. Accounts of the falls before about 1960 rarely mention bears, but even in recent decades, when poaching and other human threats have been removed, the bears were relatively sparse for a long time. Now they are gathering in larger numbers. During several summers of study at Brooks in the late 1970s, biologist Will Troyer typically saw fewer than ten bears a summer fishing the river, though two or three dozen came in September and October to catch the spawned-out fish. (Troyer thought that the river was too high in summer for successful fishing by the bears.) Today, at the peak of activity in July, more than sixty bears may use the area. Since the 1980s, human use has more than doubled. Day use—that is, visitation by people flown in for a few hours—has grown much faster, and these day users, stepping from an airplane fresh from some Alaskan city, are the hardest to educate and manage.

We met a young couple as excited as we were about being at Brooks, but still fuming about a foolish tourist stunt they'd just witnessed. Along the trail near Brooks Lodge, a pair of Italian visitors had approached within about twenty feet of a sow with young to take a picture. The sow had bluff-charged them. Apparently even this had not fully convinced them that their behavior was wrong, but they did leave the bear. Our young couple reported them to a ranger, launching the little mini-investigation that is a staple of the day-to-day process of getting along with bears at Brooks.

Shortly after we had arrived in Alaska, Bob Barbee explained to us the scale and differences of Alaska. ("Paul, there are an estimated *three million* lakes in Alaska. Nobody really knows the number for sure.") To make a point about how the state's modern society works, he said that because there are so few roads in such a huge area, people went directly from the rivers to the air. Lake Hood, on the edge of Anchorage, is the busiest seaplane base in the world; as many as eight hundred takeoffs and landings occur there on a busy summer day, and there are many other, smaller bases and airports in this part of the state. Indeed, one out of every fifty-eight Alaskans is a licensed pilot. Airplanes were in and out of many wild areas in this part of Alaska every day, providing quickie tours for people who didn't have a lot of time to spare but could afford the flight to at least get a look at all those things they had heard about.

It turned out that the Italian couple had been flown in for the day with several other people as part of a "flightseeing" tour from one of the towns across Cook Inlet. They spoke no English. When the rangers talked this over with the pilot who had brought them in, he said he didn't know they didn't understand English. He had dutifully sent them up the trail to the visitor center, where they politely sat through the orientation without understanding a thing. Then they were set loose among the people, fish, and bears to find their way to some personal vision of how best to enjoy this famous national park.

It might be wrong to call the concentrations of bears at places like Brooks Falls unnatural, but in the world of bears, such concentrations are unusual. Most bears, even those of Katmai National Park, when they aren't at salmon streams, spend most of their time alone. (Bears also gather on the Katmai coast to dig clams and, in early summer, some congregate in meadows to graze on new sedges.) They are solitary, often nocturnal. Sows are especially secretive, to protect their young from big males, which are quick to kill young bears.

But even when bears encounter each other in potentially hostile circumstances, such as over a tasty carcass, few actual fights occur. The prevailing theory is that there is no evolutionary advantage for either the winner or the loser in a fight, so why have one if they can accomplish what needs accomplishing peacefully? Bears are very slow to reproduce, and each individual in the population requires a major investment by nature just to bring it to breeding adulthood, when it can then work hard to replace itself on behalf of the next generation of bears. Exactly how these factors play out seems unclear, but the result is that bears, like people, have developed an elaborate and quite reliable way of avoiding actual violence against one another—or against any other potentially threatening species—by simply giving signs that suggest the possibility of such violence. Through a system of expressions, postures, and actions that fall just short of contact, bears can usually sort out their differences without bloodshed. (Wolves, on the other hand, which generate sizable litters of young yearly, much more regularly kill their rivals in other packs or their own.)

I first became aware of how important this caution was to bears many years ago, when doing the reading for my first bear book. After considerable searching, I made the big investment in a copy of John Holzworth's charming book *The Wild Grizzlies of Alaska* (1930). During trips to Alaska in the late 1920s, Holzworth traveled extensively on Admiralty Island with Allen Hasselborg, an extraordinary character in the history of Alaska and a veteran of many years' close contact with wild bears. Through his experiences with Hasselborg, both in the field dealing with the huge brown bears of Admiralty Island and in camp and cabin listening to Hasselborg's teachings, Holzworth changed his ideas of the scale of danger in a bear encounter.

He emphasized the bear's general unwillingness to confront humans: "Eleven times out of a dozen a grizzly, even when attacked, will retreat." Bears are rarely attacked by humans anymore, at least in places like Yellowstone and Katmai, so today's equation for the bear involves encountering humans on the one hand and avoiding them on the other. In this equation, the statistics are even more lopsided. On busy trails in national parks and other remaining sanctuaries of grizzly and brown bears today, at least those where the bears are not habituated to people, I imagine that the bears quietly leave the scene dozens of times for every one time that hikers even see them. They are very good at avoiding us, probably because they are also very good at avoiding each other.

But if a confrontation must occur, it can usually be settled without actual fighting. Bears, studied in many places, have revealed a surprisingly rich behavioral "language" of sounds and gestures and postures that usually take care of any tense moment. Charging is rarely necessary, and we long misunderstood it anyway. Holzworth, who was on Admiralty

Island especially to photograph the big bears, was surprised to learn that almost all apparent "charges" were just bluffs. Hasselborg had enough experience to be able to distinguish the serious charge from the feint, so that Holzworth got to see the proof of this. If you are a bear feeling stressed by the too-close approach of someone or something, the bluff, or false charge, is an effective way to make the point that you are upset and pose a threat. Friends of mine who have been false-charged by grizzly bears tell me that this works very well.

But Holzworth also clarified the role of the bear's personality in the false charge, pointing out that it might not be a charge at all. Bears are not known for their keen eyesight, but are universally known for their curiosity. Many quick approaches that are thought by humans to be charges are probably just a bear getting closer for a better look. (Holzworth, whose book was in good part written from the perspective of a hunter writing for hunters, also maintained that wounded bears seeming to charge were usually just trying to escape and happened to run at the hunter.)

Much of this has been known for a long time, but most of it has only begun to filter out to the public, even today when Steve Herrero's *Bear Attacks: Their Causes and Avoidance* (1985), perhaps the most important American bear book ever published, has approached best-seller status. Outdoor magazines and newspapers can still sell a lot more copies with a story about the bear that attacked than about all the bears that did not. There's nothing wrong with telling those stories as long as we can keep them in context, which we too often can't.

As biologists began to study grizzly bears, especially in the 1960s and after, the bear's way of communicating its feelings became known. Today most people who read a lot about bears tend to have a better understanding. People fortunate enough to visit one of these close-up viewing areas in Alaska experience a revelation about the nature of bears. Just north of Katmai, on the coast of Cook Inlet, is McNeil River State Game Sanctuary, where as many as sixty or seventy bears gather at one salmon-feeding area and are joined by a few humans who stand right in their midst. A beautiful book on this place, *The Way of the Grizzly* (1993), by Tom Walker and Larry Aumiller, is largely a testimonial to the peaceful coexistence of humans and giant carnivores, year after year, at this spot. In the violence scorecard of these bear-human zones, humans are way ahead of the bears. Even bluff charges are rare.

From the description we were given, it seemed clear that the female bear that charged the Italians was not curious; she was seriously annoyed. They had gotten within her threshold of tolerance, and she did her best, "speaking" in bear language, to let them know. But she shouldn't have had to bother. If people are exposed to the right training (as visitors who understand English are at Brooks), and if they take the training seriously (and even the best educators can't guarantee that), such bluff charges should almost never happen.

The Olson-Gilbert study of Brooks bears, which I described in the first chapter, analyzed just how complicated life gets for bears with all the people around. (This study is reviewed by Olson and Ronald Squibb in a handsome booklet, *Brown Bears of Brooks River* (1993), which also features the foremost published collection of color photographs of Brooks bears, taken by one of our hosts that week, Jim Gavin.) Habituation, which the researchers defined as a bear being willing to consistently tolerate humans at fifty yards' distance, was not a simple matter for any of the bears. A bear that would tolerate humans in numbers, and fairly close at the falls, might flee or otherwise react unfavorably to a smaller

number of people in a different location. During the Olson-Gilbert study period, 1988 to 1992, the bears that used Brooks River included a few (five to seven) bears that could be called habituated and perhaps twice as many (fourteen to seventeen, depending on the season) that could not.

Just why some bears habituate and some do not is not entirely clear. Shy sows teach their cubs to behave the same way, and bold sows teach their cubs boldness. But most people who have studied bears, in many places and times around the world, agree that personality also has a lot to do with each individual's way of dealing with the world, and personality is hard enough to pin down with our own species, much less with another species whose head we simply cannot get inside.

Obviously, if you are a Brooks River bear and you want to eat as many salmon as possible, habituation is an advantage, especially during the busy summer season, when there are a lot of people in your way and you need to get to the river. (According to Olson and Gilbert, a salmon like the very average ones I caught contains forty-six hundred easily digestible calories and lots of fat; by fall, those same fish, depleted of eggs, milt, and energy, are less than half as valuable as food.) Bears with less willingness to tolerate people, or with the added insecurity brought about by a need to protect cubs, just worked the edges. They made opportunistic forays into busy places when things were quieter, and spent a lot of their time dodging the human traffic.

But for all their tolerance and willingness to avoid confrontation among themselves, bears do fight, and even kill. Some of the Brooks bears we saw bore scars from past encounters, as do bears at other similar gathering places. (The bears at Yellowstone dumps in the old days were likewise sometimes scarred.) Such distinctive markings, more easily discernible and unchanging than most other physical features, often allow researchers to identify individuals from year to year when changes in color and size might otherwise make identification impossible. Periodically, some episode is witnessed by humans. In the summer of 1999, one of the largest dominant males at the falls caught and killed a cub, then ate it within view of a platform full of shocked and fascinated visitors.

Most of the time, such rare action in the life of the bear takes place out of view. A sow known to have two cubs suddenly has only one, or a bear appears with a raw wound. Perhaps the most famous of recent bears at Brooks, known as Diver for his entertaining skill at completely submerging to swim after salmon, is now about thirty years old (Troyer knew him as an adult bear in the 1970s), quite an age for a wild bear. In 1988, when he returned to the river for the salmon run, he sported a large, fresh gash on his back, but was undaunted and still a leading presence among the fishing bears. In 1991, according to the park service's annually updated booklet, *Bear Facts*, Diver was seen swimming around near the footbridge, which puzzled observers because no salmon had arrived yet;

94

then "the great bear emerged with a full grown beaver in his powerful jaws and headed to the river bank to enjoy his catch." Life is exciting and often dangerous for these animals, even without weaving their way through people.

Late in the morning, I was fishing the river just upstream around the first bend from the pontoon bridge. There were only a few fishermen around. Marsha had joined Kate, a Young American Conservation Corps staffer who was the platform monitor at the time, on the platform.

The ranger or other staff member on the platform is not responsible for all of us within sight. They are not required or expected to serve as spotter for us, and the park service is not offering a guaranteed safe experience. This is emphasized in the park brochures. The monitors keep track of traffic back and forth to the falls and do a lot of what the park service calls "interpretation," and what the rest of the world calls "education." To whatever extent they can, they also keep an eye out for bears. If a bear does appear, the platform person will try to let fishermen and anyone else in the area know, and encourage them to come to the platform if the bear gets too close. (There is no loudspeaker for this purpose, and I hope such an ugly intrusion is never added to the scene.) During our visit, the full complement of summer bears was not yet in residence. Everyone we spoke with agreed that when thirty or more bears are moving around the narrow band of land along the river between the bridge and the falls, a special kind of madness descends on Brooks, and everyone is very busy and very alert. Not having experienced that higher form of contained hysteria, I thought I was about as alert as I could get.

I found a nice group of salmon, rolling easily in the slow current near shore. Fishing for them aimed me away from the platform, but I still looked around a lot. When not looking around, I could make easy casts of about thirty feet, drifting the fly past several active fish. As they gave the fly a look or just did that mysterious porpoising roll that so many freshly arrived salmon seem to favor, their motions roiled the surface in circular, plate-size upwellings that slid away and dissipated. These little signs of active fish drive both fishermen and bears a little crazy.

There had been bears around earlier. When we arrived, a little after eleven o'clock, a sow and a cub, which we would see at the bridge every day from then on, were fooling around in the water just upstream of the bridge. Marsha and I, coming from our quarters over on Brooks Lake, had walked right past the platform's back end on our way to the bridge. There were a couple well-outfitted young fly fishermen in full regalia standing and talking by the platform's back ramp. We walked right past them and nearly to the bridge before someone on the platform called down to us to stop. There were bears out, we were told, and we should get up on the platform right away. As we went back to the ramp, I wanted to stop and ask the idiot fishermen why they had let us walk right past without warning us, but I was gradually realizing that a disappointing part of Brooks's social scene was a kind of bravado disregard—a hip, too-cool-to-be-awestruck diffidence—for such niceties among a few visitors, almost invariably male, who considered themselves more savvy about all this and just a little above the rules.

We stood on the platform for quite a while, taking a few more pictures and waiting for the bears to move on. This was probably the first time we also heard complaints about bears being "in the way." As unimaginable as it might seem to someone who dreams hopelessly of finally being in a place like this, there were fishermen actually grumbling that the bears were keeping them from fishing. I thought at the time that one of the greatest fishing stories I could ever hope to bore my friends back home with would be "Let me tell you about the time I had to leave the river and go hide until these huge Alaskan brown bears left." Fishing couldn't possibly be better without that experience than with it.

Later, along that quiet, grass-lined bank, the hooking was also very good. I had two or three fish on, including some that I was confident were fair-hooked, but they escaped quickly. I checked the hook to make sure the point hadn't been dulled against a rock or somehow gotten twisted too far open to hold, and continued casting. I hooked another fish, this time firmly. It didn't fight as hard as some of the others, but made a couple of respectable runs before I managed to pull it in close. I could plainly see the bright green of Bill's little salmon fly attached to the fish's front end; it was fair-hooked.

I was deliberating whether to horse it in and risk losing it by rushing things, or just hold it there for a moment to see if it would take off for another run, when I noticed that a guide was walking through the high grass, coming up to the other bank of the stream behind me. He was leading a group of four anglers. I recognized him as one of the lodge's young guides, a well-mannered young man who seemed to try to take good care of his people whether they knew what they were doing or not.

It might seem a flaw in my story that I could be concentrating so hard on this salmon I was just then playing and still know that some people were approaching from directly behind me. I could use the excuse that I saw the people because even with a fish on I didn't stop looking around frequently for bears, but in fact I had only been doing what any sensible fisherman would do under the circumstances—looking around to make sure that everybody could see me catching my fish. Because of the distance, I couldn't quite tell what they were doing on the platform, but I hoped that Marsha was watching.

My salmon drifted off downstream a short distance, pulling line from the reel in slow spurts. I let it go while I turned to speak with the guide, who was now standing along the far shore of the river behind me. We were close enough that I didn't have to raise my voice to tell him—with some misgivings about being so good a sport about sharing—that I had found a good spot and that the fish were strung out all along in here. He turned to tell his four clients that they should wade across and fish downstream from this gentleman, but before any of them reached the bank, I could see that his attention had been caught by something downstream. I followed his line of vision and saw the head of a large brown bear poking up through the higher bank grass perhaps seventy-five feet downstream of me. Again, showing consistency if no inspiration, my first reaction was to say, "Oh shit."

In February 1986, *National Geographic* published a long article by Douglas Chadwick on grizzly bear conservation. It included a pair of pictures of the pioneering grizzly bear researcher John Craighead, fishing for salmon at Brooks River. In the first picture, Craighead's back is to the camera as he attempts to reel in a struggling fish, which a brown bear is eyeing enthusiastically from shore. In the second picture, Craighead is energetically attempting to break the line, which now proceeds right to the bear, which jumped in and grabbed the fish. The caption reads that "Craighead broke the line . . . averting a potentially hazardous encounter." True enough, but the incident certainly provided some on-the-job training for the bear, which couldn't have failed to notice that fishermen can make it a lot easier to catch salmon.

At least some of the Brooks bears have learned to listen for the sound of fish jumping and struggling when hooked, perhaps even for the sound of fly reels giving line with that loud, ratchety whine when the fish makes a good run. I don't know if any of this had attracted the bear to me, but I was at risk of violating one of the most passionately expressed rules at Brooks: Whatever you do, don't feed your fish to a bear. If you're playing a fish and a bear approaches, you absolutely must avoid letting that bear get the fish and therefore learning to associate the fish so directly with fishermen.

With my eyes on the bear, which walked along the bank in my direction, I started backing away, out into the middle of the river and toward the guide, who had stopped his clients from getting in the water. My fish was now hanging downstream more or less even with the bear. I asked the guide if he thought I should break the fish off. He wasn't sure, but he didn't think I needed to yet. I, on the other hand, thought I needed to very badly, so I did. Pointing the rod directly at the fish, and grabbing the rod and line together just above the handle, I pulled upstream until the leader parted and the line came zinging back toward me. (Breaking off the fish by hauling back on the rod like you are actually trying to bring the fish toward you is a good way to break the rod.) As soon as the fish was off, I hurried out of the water, past the guide and his milling anglers, and made my way across the bridge to the platform. The bear ambled on upstream, and in a few minutes fishing resumed, but I was done for a while.

At the platform, Marsha and Kate assured me that they had both been yelling at me as loud as they could. From their high angle, they could see the bear emerge from the forest and work his way up the shore. Low in the water, I couldn't see anything until he was close. I objected to Kate that she needed to work on her projection, and explained that I had almost just had lunch with that bear, but I knew none of that was her fault. I was supposed to be responsible here.

Responsibility has a lot to do with the management debates at Brooks. The National Park Service's leadership, veterans of many ugly situations in which visitors are hurt, does not want such an awful thing to happen, or the bear to pay the price when it does, or to get taken to court for negligence. Ultimately, in the eyes of the public and the courts, the National Park Service is responsible for making things work. It is responsible for making sure the bears have access to the fish, and making sure people don't get hurt or killed. The situation at Brooks, with such intimate and exciting mixings of people and bears, has deeply troubled park service leaders for years. Out of this uneasiness has come a plan for a major overhaul of the whole facility at Brooks, and the controversy over this facility is in a way the story of competing interests in Alaska, another small, local version of what Henry and I heard from our first Alaskan. In this controversy, some contestants insist that the park service owes a greater responsibility to the bears, not only for the welfare of the bears, but also for the benefit of the people who enjoy them. Other contestants maintain that the park service owes greater responsibility to the region's struggling business interests, more or less arguing that those business interests will do well by both bears and the people.

Brooks is unlike other popular bear-viewing areas in Alaska in that the people are allowed free run of the bears' neighborhood. At the falls on McNeil River, for example, small groups of people, selected by lottery, are led by a staff member along a single trail to specific viewing areas on the ground at the falls (there is no viewing platform); they have been moving exactly like this for so many years that a lot of bears have spent their entire adult lives knowing precisely where the people will and won't be. The people are taught how to move, and how to be least intrusive while there. By this, the bears learn trust and tolerance.

The result has been sensational. Some bears will saunter right up and nurse their cubs within a few yards of the ecstatic viewers. In more than two decades, nobody has been hurt, and no bear has been killed. As at Brooks, bears show different levels of habituation. Some will fish only on the opposite side of the river from the people; others will cozy right up to them.

For many years, Brooks's managers, their scientific advisors, and some of their constituency groups have recognized the need to more aggressively sort out people and bears, not only for the safety of the people, but also to give the bears the assurances they need that their turf is secure. This is made all the more difficult because Brooks was developed as a fishing lodge long before the bears were an attraction. Unlike the other popular Alaskan bear-viewing areas, there is a sizable visitor facility—lodge, cabins, staff housing, visitor center, campground—right in the middle of everything. The beach past the campground and lodge is a major bear travel route, and bears are constantly wandering around among the buildings. At McNeil River, by contrast, visitors camp in a tiny, restricted area well away from the falls and of little interest to bears. There are only a couple of very small and uninteresting administrative cabins anywhere nearby.

But there is much more at stake here even than the bears. One of the great changes to come over the National Park Service and its sister land-management agencies in recent decades is a finer commitment to the preservation of cultural resources, even those in the midst of great natural resources. In many national parks originally established as "nature parks," there are now known to be considerable evidences of both prehistoric and historical human activities. These evidences, grouped under the label of cultural resources, range from tiny "lithic scatters," where a thousand years ago someone sat for a few moments and repaired a projectile point, to the warehouse-size hotels in Yosemite, Yellowstone, Glacier, and other parks, some more than a century old and repositories of great quantities of American tradition, folklore, and beloved memory. All these cultural resources are protected by powerful laws that require federal agencies to care for them as an integral part of the setting.

Over the past forty years at Brooks, archaeologists (the most notable must be Dan Dumond of the University of Oregon, who has been productive throughout this period) have discovered and analyzed a wonderful example of such resources. The Brooks River corridor seems to have been occupied quite regularly for at least the past forty-five hundred years. National Park Service archaeologist Patricia McClenahan evoked some of the excitement of these discoveries in her 1989 nomination of the site for the National Register of Historic Places:

> Here at Brooks River can be found a vast amount of prehistoric cultural remains, evident at 20 archeological sites with a total of some 960 depressions, many thought to be remains of substantial semisubterranean houses. These sites are strikingly concentrated in a relatively small area on ridges and terraces overlooking the 2.5 kilometer-long Brooks River and the nearby shores of Brooks and Naknek Lakes. A natural feature of particular importance is picturesque Brooks Falls, where large numbers of fish collect in the natural pool there while attempting to surmount the falls and continue upstream.

McClenahan's inclusion of the river and the falls in this description was not whimsy or casual travelogue. In the world of cultural resource preservation, an archaeological site is not just a hole in the ground or a few crumbling walls; it is part of a larger place, known in professional parlance as a cultural landscape. An understanding of the immediate area of the site—ruined cabin, stone quarry, petroglyph, or whatever it may be—is impossible without reference to where it sits. Thus is the entire corridor of Brooks River appropriated by another bureaucratic interest group—the cultural resource specialists and their large public constituencies—as "theirs." The land, the river, the falls, and in some real way even the fish all represent values that need our care for this new set of cultural reasons. The old "natural" resource has been redefined to embrace these reasons. In the view of modern managers and their cultural resource professionals, this is done for the good of the resource; the good of the public, who should have a chance to benefit from the archaeological sites, just as they benefit from the bears; and, it is hoped, for the good of the descendants of the people who occupied this area for so long and left such important evidence of their lives in the ground. Back from the north shore of the river, accessible by a nice trail and regularly visited by park rangers leading guided tours, a *barabara,* or pit house, has been excavated and restored to show how people lived here a thousand years ago. To protect the open pit and its unroofed frame structure, a small log cabin was built around the site. The bears have been chewing on its corners.

But even McClenahan's description may not do justice to what is there, and how it affects modern managers trying to direct the care of Brooks. Twenty sites with 960 depressions have been identified so far. On a map of their distribution, many things become clear. Everywhere you walk, you are liable to be treading on an archaeological treasure. The puzzlingly lumpy contours of Scary Hill are revealed as the remains of ancient pit houses. If you seek a deeper connection with this place, consider that you will also be walking among the ghosts of all the bears, salmon, and people who have been converging on this place for the last few millennia.

But if you care about the preservation of natural and archaeological wonders, the situation is also a kind of nightmare. The entire development at Brooks, so long in coming and representing such a laborious struggle for funds, public attention, and sense of direction, is now judged by hindsight to have been a big mistake. Fifty years ago, the National Park

Service, anxious to get something going in Katmai visitation, had every reason to welcome the development of these facilities at Brooks. But values and interests change. All these buildings, public and personal investments of great sacrifice, have been laid over a cultural site of such significance that if it were discovered today with no development on top of it, a proposal for such a development would be met with laughter, if not indignation. I could say that it is the archaeological equivalent of having painted over a Rembrandt, but it might be more accurate to say that it is the equivalent of just doodling on the Rembrandt with crayons. Even if it weren't for the bear-people management problems at Brooks, this would be cause for serious consideration of moving the development.

By the early 1980s, the park service's specialists and managers were looking to the day that all facilities at Brooks could be relocated to better protect bears, visitors, cultural resources, and the overall quality of the visitor experience. In a long and arduous process involving massive amounts of conversation, study, public involvement, and soul-searching, the *Final Development Plan, Environmental Impact Statement* was published by the National Park Service in 1996, proposing to move all of the facilities north of the river, including the lodge, cabins, residences, visitor center, and campground, to various sites a mile or more back from the south side of the river. Trails to bear-viewing areas would be rerouted away from as many sensitive archaeological sites (like Scary Hill) as possible. Tighter restrictions and seasonal closures on fishing would pretty much eliminate encounters like mine with the bear that was curious about the salmon on my line.

Alaska's highest political powers have been very active in this process. In 1998, Alaska Senator Ted Stevens saw to it that legislation was passed preventing the National Park Service from in any way placing "caps" on the number of visitors who could go to Brooks on a given day. In late 1999, Stevens pulled from the appropriations budget the six million dollars that the park service expected to spend on the relocation in 2000 because, according to one of the senator's aides, the plan was not "visitor-friendly." The park service's cautious desire to restrict the movements and numbers of visitors is anathema to Alaskans who want recreational commerce to flourish and continue to grow. Stevens's adversaries, including the recently formed Friends of Katmai, continue to echo park staff concerns about the mounting pressure of more people and more bears at Brooks. Late in 1998, after our visit, bears broke into nineteen buildings, doing considerable damage in an action that Friends of Katmai saw as proof of growing stress between bears and people. It was probably also reflective of the failed salmon run of the summer. It was certainly an indication of some bears behaving as they had rarely behaved before, and perhaps that is warning enough that close attention must be paid.

As with previous generations in the struggle to define Katmai's future, the senator's budgetary withdrawal was only the latest round in a long negotiating process that has pitted the park service's leaders and the conservation community against him and the more commercial interests he represents. As chairman of the Senate Appropriations Committee, the senator holds a lot of cards in this game and, like his fellow Alaskans, Senator Frank Murkowski and Congressman Don Young, is widely regarded among environmental activists as an ogre. In 1969, when he was a brand new senator, Stevens was among the last public officials to seriously threaten abolishing Katmai National Monument. In 1983, he introduced a bill to the Senate that would have opened most Alaskan national parks and monuments to public sport hunting. But he is elected again and again, presumably because Alaskans think he is doing a good job. (One of his local nicknames is the "uncrowned king of Alaska.") Indeed, in the case of Katmai, it looks to me as though he ably, perhaps even brilliantly, represents the polished and informed versions of the positions held by that first Alaskan who lectured Henry and me on what was wrong with us and our employers.

Presumably, the process will continue to klunk along. All the interests, all the citizens, journalists, and advocacy groups with their staffs and lawyers and publications and memberships—that is, all of us who former U.S. Forest Service chief Jack Ward Thomas described as the "Conflict Industry"—will keep expressing ourselves and exercising our rights to speak, pressure, and litigate. With luck, and with the admirable persistence that the most important parties have shown at communicating even when they disagree, it seems entirely possible that eventually people and bears will be more clearly separated than they are now, and that the other resources at Brooks will be better served. But as I read the record of this debate, and especially the impassioned positions taken by some of the most vocal and influential parties, I too often hear our abysmally misinformed roadside Alaskan holding forth.

Later in the afternoon, I tried to return to the grassy bank to resume my attentions on that group of fish, but a crew of six loud sportsmen had claimed the whole stretch. It was not the group accompanied by the guide; it was another bunch, to whom I had injudiciously described the place when Marsha and I were eating lunch under the cache beside the visitor center. It is an odd part of fishing that for all its reputation as Izaak

Walton's "quiet man's recreation," it involves so much racket. As I worked my way downstream toward the deep bend right above the bridge, one of these chaps hooked a fish, and his bellows and whoops might have been audible at the falls.

At the next pool, a man and his teenage son had the good spot, from which they could cast over the largest pod of salmon I had yet seen, a hundred or so holding in a loose, shifting cloud over the pale river bottom. Both fishermen and fish were quite tolerant of my presence. The boy was regularly snagging salmon, hauling back on each one with a soprano grunt, playing them for a minute or so, and then unaccountably losing them. I never saw him land one, but he was having a great time. I struck up a conversation with his father, who explained that they had been coming here for many years, and he had never seen the fishing so poor. These things are all a matter of scale, and I am sure that from his perspective, this luxurious gob of big fish was just a shadow of his memories.

Then another bear came by, entering the area from the direction of the lodge. It crossed the footbridge, passed directly in front of the platform, and continued upstream along the shore until it was directly across the water from us, perhaps sixty yards off. A louder voice now occupied the platform, and as soon as the bear appeared, the word came down, "Fishermen, lines out of the water!" This was the early-warning stage of a bear's approach, given just to prepare you for other movements if necessary, to save you the time it took to retrieve your line, and to prevent an untimely hookup with a splashing salmon that might attract the bear.

The father and his son brought in their lines. We were all about knee-deep in the river. The son had gone upstream toward the bellowers, but the father was still downstream from me, which meant he was about fifteen yards closer to the bear than I was when he put on one of the most interesting displays of what I was now recognizing as the local "not-afraid-of-a-lousy-bear cool" I had seen. I was not yet accustomed enough to the bears to take my eyes off them even if they weren't close, but this man turned his back on the bear and for the next ten or fifteen minutes determinedly stared off in the opposite direction. There really was nothing up there to see, except eight or ten other people all watching the bear.

It was an affectation, of course—a showing off for all the other people who had to look past him to see the bear. It said, "I've been here before, and this doesn't impress me. Ho-hum." It said other things, as well, but by this time I was getting a little tired of my own judgmental reactions against my fellow sportsmen. After the bear left, so did I.

Marsha was ready to go too, so we went to the falls. It was crowded at the platform, but it was somewhat more benign an atmosphere than at one point on Tuesday when a tall, well-dressed, dignified tourist stank so intensely that even Alaska couldn't freshen up the atmosphere around him, and we were hard put to escape in the close quarters of the

group. The magic of the place was still powerful, but contemplating social complications was tiring. Sometimes nature is hard to share. It was rainy, and we were discontented and a little hungry.

Then a huge brown bear walked right past the front of the platform, and we looked directly down on that luxurious coat and sofa-size expanse of shoulder and back and admired him for the masterpiece he was. It may have been early in the season, and he may have had hundreds of pounds to gain before fall, but already he was, like Chaucer's hedonistic monk, "a fine fat patrician, in prime condition."

We also got our first good look at Diver doing his famous act. He waded out to the deeper water below the falls, then seemed to either step in over his depth or crouch down as part of his swimming motion. He disappeared entirely under the foam, sometimes coming up only enough for his ears or shoulders to show. For a while there was just a briefcase-size patch of bedraggled fur that appeared to be floating independently around in the pool, unattached to a big bear. We didn't see him bring up a fish, but when he finally waded out of the deep pool and water was sluicing off his sides, he braced his feet on the rocky streambed and shook himself dry just like an immense brown dog.

A Helluva Job

We are awaiting death at any moment. Of course do not be alarmed.
—Ivan Orloff, writing to his wife from the Katmai coast during the volcanic eruptions, June 9, 1912

In the morning, ranger-naturalist Monte Crooks and his wife, Sue, came by in the park's Suburban and took Marsha and me out to the Valley of Ten Thousand Smokes. The twenty-three-mile drive, on a well-maintained gravel road, reminded me of the bus ride through Denali. Both roads are generally restricted to tour buses and administrative traffic. Katmai has one bus making one round-trip a day, compared with the fleet of buses at Denali, but the effect of controlled access is the same. More important, both are unaccompanied by other human disturbances along the way. Except for the rare and small administrative structure, for miles at a stretch there is nothing at the edge of the road but an exceptionally real Alaska—for all you might guess, it reaches on beyond the mountainous horizon all the way around and comes up behind you against the road's other edge.

There aren't even very many trails. As in Denali, except near developments where human traffic is heavy enough to need some funneling just for the sake of the local vegetation, you are encouraged to go cross-country as you see fit. With so few visitors per year, this is a nice system. It not only leaves the hiker more freedom for spontaneity, it also spreads out the use and leaves little trace of the passage of people. It is in good part the luxury of a small visitation, though. If a park, such as Yellowstone, Great Smoky Mountains, Grand Canyon, Yosemite, and others, receives millions of visitors, and managers want to keep most of the backcountry untrampled, then there is no choice but to build and maintain substantial trails. The Old Faithful area of Yellowstone gets more visitors in three summer days than Katmai National Park and Preserve gets in an entire season.

We stopped for a look at Margot Falls, on the list of lesser marvels that park service planners hope eventually to make somewhat more accessible. For now, there is a barely discernible path, the kind that in the park service is known as a "social trail"—one made by visitors doing something visitors just wanted to do, rather than an officially maintained route that might even appear on maps. It's a few minutes through the brush to a small and somewhat woozy little overlook among the rocks on the edge of a narrow, forested canyon.

The falls is lovely, almost smothered by its green surroundings. More a cascade, really, it boils and twists solid white down through a dark rock gorge just like many in Yellowstone, and more in Glacier, that remind me how important scale is in our perception of nature. In the monumental scale of the local scenery, this falls is a minor treat, good for a thirty-minute break in the bus ride from Brooks, but not likely to make the postcards sent home. Anywhere on the Great Plains it would justify a sizable state park, with attendant curio shops, fast food, and a dubious but well-marketed legend about suicidal Indian lovers.

There are three river fords on the way to the valley, one of them broad and deep enough to be exciting to the uninitiated, the others just novel. At a small, shady crossing on our way out, just as the stream came into view, a wolf walked onto the road in front of us. It was the only one I saw in Alaska. Unlike the probable coyote that the Denali bus driver said was a wolf, there was no doubt about this animal. It had all the right moves, the rangy, almost lanky dimensions, and a mottled pale coat of no particular colors. It stood in the road for a moment watching us approach with those bright, opportunistic eyes. Wild herbivores tend to look at you with concern, as if deciding which way to run, but carnivores give you a more appraising look. They too are deciding which way to run, but also seem to be wondering how you'd taste. There was something dead, or at least a ratty chunk of something dead, swinging limp from the wolf's mouth. If the dead thing wasn't just a floppy piece of some larger dead thing, it might have been a ptarmigan, but the wolf loped on into the brush before we could get close enough to tell.

You know you're in a magical place—or that you are in the right frame of mind to appreciate the magic that is latent in any place—when it occurs to you that a sudden and wonderful moment like this is a great addition to your day but wasn't really necessary.

In a rough line from Mount Spurr, west of Anchorage, down the Alaskan Peninsula about eight hundred miles, and then swinging out another thousand miles through the two hundred-odd islands of the Aleutians, there are about eighty volcanoes. In the past two and a half centuries, perhaps half of these volcanoes have been reported to erupt, some several times. In good part because of the volcanic activity, the peninsula's most pronounced feature is the chain of mountains that runs along its south shore. Reporting on his studies there in the 1920s and 1930s, pioneering Alaska biologist Olaus Murie described the whole peninsula in a way that well characterizes Katmai country:

> The north shore of the Alaskan Peninsula shelves off gradually into the shallow waters of the Bering Sea, forming a low coastal plain with a relatively even coastline. However, farther inland, the land rises to the rugged Alaskan Range, which runs the length of the Peninsula, and, on the south side, breaks off into the deeper water of the North Pacific.

Murie could also have been speaking directly about Katmai when he said that "a striking feature of the Aleutian climate is the prevalence of foggy or cloudy weather, the abundance of rain in the summer, and the frequent violent winds that arise suddenly and unexpectedly."

Brooks River, its bears, and its salmon had nothing to do with the creation of Katmai National Monument in 1918. The monument was largely the doing of a few Department of the Interior officials and the energetic executives of the National Geographic Society, all of whom were concerned with preserving and memorializing the site of a titanic volcanic event that occurred in 1912 but whose character and extent were only vaguely understood at the time.

Relatively few people, most of them native, lived within the current park boundaries in 1912. Small, isolated groups of people occupied a few sites along the coast of Shelikoff Strait just south of the mountain range, and others fished and hunted in the Naknek Lake watershed. Not counting sailors in a few passing ships farther off, there may have been no more than fifty people available to witness the eruptions even from a distance of ten or twenty miles.

Area residents were not unaccustomed to seismic activity. They probably had local traditions relating to what had been going on for centuries in the region. In 1898 geologist and later mountain namesake Josiah Spurr traveled through the present park area, where he felt earthquakes and was assured by natives that at least one of the nearby volcanoes was then intermittently active enough to release smoke. But in the first week of June 1912, the premonitory rumblings were so exceptional that most people fled to the coasts. The village of Savonoski, at the head of the Iliuk Arm of Naknek Lake about seventeen miles east of Brooks River, was the largest community in the present park area, but because the salmon canneries over on the Bristol Bay coast were hiring right then, most of its hundred or so inhabitants were already at the fishing village of Naknek, sixty miles farther from the mountains. When the eruption began, the remaining families at Savonoski made a harrowing escape to Naknek in small boats. On the other side of the mountains, along the peninsula coast and on the nearby islands, hundreds of people were evacuated by a few local vessels, with the loss of only one life, that of a tubercular elderly woman who died from either the effects of the ash-filled air or the stress of the emergency.

Even if close enough, few of these people were in a position to actually witness the eruptions. The volcanoes were obscured behind nearer ranges and foothills, and once the event was well under way, towering columns of black smoke and dense falls of ash obscured distant views anyway. But the overall effects were more easy to quantify.

Historian John Hussey, in his irreplaceable *Embattled Katmai: A History of Katmai National Monument* (1971), has done the most thorough recent job of reviewing the firsthand local, regional, and global accounts. The sound of the initial major explosion on June 6 was heard in Fairbanks, 500 miles to the north; Dawson City, 650 miles northeast; and Juneau, 750 miles east. The several cubic miles of material that were thrown into the sky during the sixty hours of greatest eruptive activity laid a foot of ash on an area of 3,000 square miles, and at least an inch of ash on 30,000 square miles. Sulfuric acid produced by the airborne ash ruined clothes hanging on lines in Vancouver, British Columbia, 1,500 miles south. According to Hussey, "By August 5, 1912, the sulphur in the air had spread far enough to tarnish the mirrors at the Mount Wilson Observatory in Southern California." Over the next several months, these stupendous quantities of dust were lofted clear around the planet, causing a slight temperature decline through the Northern Hemisphere. It was, in the words of one native observer, a "Helluva job."

Starting in 1913, botanist Robert Griggs made a series of visits to the area to study the aftereffects of the eruptions. It may seem odd that a botanist should become the premier authority and explorer of this volcanic region, but in his first visits, he was at least as attracted to the botanical opportunities. As in other great volcanic events, much of the landscape is so seared by the ash and heat that it presents an essentially vacant habitat to all comers. The character and pace of recolonization of such a place by plants is fascinating, and scientists get relatively few opportunities to study the process. Griggs ended up writing mostly about the volcanoes, but intermittently, among his numerous publications on the study and exploration of the volcanic scene, Griggs did report on his ecological studies of the revegetation process that he first went to Alaska to study.

In 1913 Griggs visited Kodiak Island, which forms the south coast of Shelikof Strait, thirty or forty miles from the Katmai coast on the peninsula. He found deep drifts of ash partly burying houses at the town of Kodiak, one hundred miles east of the volcanoes. The grainy, indistinct black and white photographs of these ashfalls and related slides, published in a series of *National Geographic* articles in the teens, show what appear to be oddly dense snowdrifts.

In 1915 his small party returned to the area, this time reaching Katmai village on the coast and even hiking some way up the Katmai Valley toward Katmai Pass. The men walked through a blasted landscape covered with immense amounts of ash. Entire river drainages and forests were smothered in the mud and silt of the floods that followed the eruptions. Weird erosion channels, skeletal remains of trees, and immense boulders rolled long distances by the floods brought home to *National Geographic* readers the rawness of the place, and further demonstrated the colossal power of the eruption. Tantalized by all this, in 1916 Griggs and his group returned again and finally crossed Katmai Pass, the historic and prehistoric travel route across the mountain range. The volcanic range stretched east and west from the pass as he looked down the slope to the northwest, into what would become the foremost attraction and wonder of the Katmai area for many years, the Valley of Ten Thousand Smokes. He had seen a few steam vents, known as fumaroles, and hot spots on the climb, but nothing had prepared him for this.

> The sight that flashed into view as we surmounted the hillock was one of the most amazing visions ever beheld by mortal eye. The whole valley as far as the eye could reach was full of hundreds, no

thousands—literally tens of thousands—of smokes curling up from its fissured floor.

From our position they looked as small as the little fumaroles near by, but realizing something of their distance we knew many of them must be gigantic. Some were sending up columns of steam which rose a thousand feet before dissolving.

After a careful estimate, we judged there must be a thousand whose columns exceeded 500 feet. A dozen miles away the valley turned behind a blue mountain in the distance. Plainly the smokes extended that far. How much farther we could not tell.

The first glance was enough to assure us that we had stumbled into another Yellowstone Park—unseen and unsuspected by white man and native alike until this hour.

For all their other notable finds, this valley became the centerpiece of scientific research, and the primary justification for the creation of the monument in 1918. Much like Yellowstone following its creation in 1872, for many years few people saw this new marvel for themselves. They relied on descriptions, artwork, and photographs brought back by hardy adventurers whose own exploits, often genuinely daring and perilous, just heightened the sense of wonder felt by faraway admirers of nature at its most unearthly and wild. Reading Griggs's accounts of his trips into the valley in *National Geographic* and in his eminently desirable book *The Valley of Ten Thousand Smokes* (1922), it is difficult not to feel the effect that that wonder must have had on early-twentieth-century Americans. Just when it was possible to believe that the planet was running out of new mysteries, here came this amazing story out of Alaska.

With the National Geographic Society's unique gift for capturing the bizarre and unexpected, these publications, as well as Society film footage of a Griggs expedition, successfully contrasted this strange region with everything familiar. The fourfold panoramic frontispiece in Griggs's book is a four-mile-wide view of a steaming, fissured valley. A single man stands near his tent in the foreground and provides scale for the hundreds of steam columns, some winding crookedly up through intermittent breezes, others snaking along the ground for hundreds of yards. Colored photographs—looking suspiciously doctored and untrustworthy to the modern eye—show vividly pink and yellow mudflows and vent fields. Huge pumice boulders that weighed almost nothing are carried around by expedition members in mock herculean labors. In some spruce trees near Kodiak, moss caught and held large clumps of falling ash like a wet spring snow, then engulfed the ash in a new growth of moss, leaving the trees with long, absurdly bulbous branches much thicker on the ends than near the trunk. Film sequences in the valley show expedition members using a frying pan with a handle several feet long to fry bacon over a steam vent; nestling a pot of beans into a convenient bank of superheated soil; sliding a small bar of lead over a vent, which quickly melted it; digging through black, wind-borne layers of ash at the edge of the valley to the bright snow underneath; tossing water from a coffeepot into the uprush of heat from a vent to show how the water instantly flashed into steam before falling; climbing down a rope into a steaming crater, disappearing now and then behind the clouds of steam belching from this hole that is quite clearly some back door to hell.

Even the still-not-famous bears got into the act. Griggs reported that bears, perhaps attracted by the warmth, created their own steam vents:

In one of the steaming areas [botanist Paul] Hagelbarger found a place where the hot ground had apparently excited the bear's curiosity, for he had dug into it until he started a small fumarole of his own. The appearance of a cloud of steam under his claws as he broke into the hot crust must have given him a great surprise. It did not scare him away, however, for not satisfied with a single experiment, he tried again in several places, each time digging down until he started the steam before turning away.

Again and again, the uniqueness—the world-class weirdness and therefore importance—of the place was emphasized. And, again and again, to my great interest, comparisons were drawn to Yellowstone. With the hyperbole of a used-car salesman in a loud sport coat, Griggs made the comparison right out:

> The total length of all of these smoking valleys is 32 miles. The area is 70 square miles, the average width being 2 miles. . . .
>
> With these dimensions at hand, it will be interesting to compare the valley with the Yellowstone Park. In the Yellowstone there are about 4,000 hot springs and a hundred geysers scattered over an area of some 3,000 square miles. The geysers, which are the most interesting feature, occur in several isolated geyser basins, whose total area is hardly 20 square miles. The largest of the geysers, which play but seldom, shoot up a column scarcely 300 feet in height. The column of Old Faithful, which is the only geyser the tourist can count on seeing in action, is about 100 feet high.

In the Alaskan valley [the Valley of Ten Thousand Smokes] there are in constant action thousands of vents whose columns exceed that figure. The columns of several of the largest vents may, when conditions are right, ascend more than 5,000 feet into the air or, under the influence of the winds which sweep the valley, trail along the ground for two or three miles.

Though none of this may have overstated the magnificence of the Valley of Ten Thousand Smokes, it consistently understated that of Yellowstone. But his point was well taken. The Alaskan valley did put on a far grander steam show than any of Yellowstone's geothermal basins could in even the coldest weather, when they produce many thick, towering columns of steam. The valley was really something.

It is part of national park tradition, both among park service people and among writers who cover park stories, to compare things to Yellowstone. As the oldest and most famous of American national parks, Yellowstone has been made a kind of standard against which others are measured, another Guinness Book way of reducing things to a simplistic scale for a personal frame of reference and the convenience of public consumption. When the new Alaskan parks were created in 1980, their sizes were reflexively and quite favorably measured against that of Yellowstone, presumably because it is a place that the public is more familiar with. In my readings about Katmai, I have been struck by how often this comparison seemed important for some reason or other. But the most intriguing connection between Yellowstone and Katmai came about during the short, successful effort to preserve the latter.

Because the leaders of the brand new National Park Service, created in 1916, were leery of arousing too much local objection so soon after the 1917 creation of Mount McKinley National Park, they urged that Katmai be made a national monument, a vague and somewhat less threatening land classification that at least implied greater access to local commerce. On September 24, 1918, President Woodrow Wilson dutifully signed the proclamation creating the monument. Wilson's proclamation emphasized the scientific interest that the volcanic region on the Alaska Peninsula generated, singling out Mount Katmai as of "importance in the study of volcanism, inasmuch as its eruption of June, 1912, was one of excessive violence." It emphasized both the ongoing scientific values of the area and its interest to "visitors," presumably tourists. It said that the grand scale of the scene would arouse "emotions of wonder at the inspiring spectacles, thus affording inspiration to patriotism and the study of nature." And—in an eyebrow-raising additional justification, in case the others weren't enough—it singled out the Valley of Ten Thousand Smokes as especially important as "a possible future geyser field, in distinction from the present dying geyser field of the Yellowstone."

When I first read that Katmai was partly justified on the grounds that Yellowstone's geothermal activity was dying out, it rang a faint mental bell and sent me looking through old publication files in Yellowstone. Indeed, in the 1890s and for some years after, there was a flurry of alarm, both in the popular press and in the scientific literature, that Yellowstone's geysers were fading. Looking back on it from a century later, with some of the still-robust Yellowstone geothermal activity visible out my window as I write, it is perhaps too easy to be cynical about this dark view that some early Yellowstone writers took. I've met or read any number of old-timers who revisited Yellowstone after many years, and they tend to see the geothermal features as smaller, just as we are shocked at how small our childhood haunts are when we return to them. "It ain't like it used to be" is a fond lament of some truth, but it is also a testament to poorly remembered better days.

The quarter century from Yellowstone National Park's creation in 1872 to the 1890s was just long enough for the minds of that first generation of visitors to work their subtle embellishments on memories. Add to that the inherent undependability of all geothermal features—including even Old Faithful, which has sometimes slowed its average eruption interval over the past century, and never did erupt "on the hour"—and it was not hard to find "proof" of decline among specific features. So there was, indeed, a fear if not a conviction that Yellowstone wasn't going to last.

What makes this idea—that Katmai could be a replacement for Yellowstone—so entertaining and important is that it was precisely wrong. Decade after decade, Yellowstone has steamed, gurgled, and spouted on, while in a very short time, Katmai calmed down with hardly a puff. This is not to the credit of Yellowstone or the discredit of Katmai; it's just how their geological fortunes worked out.

But to some who watched the rapid decline of the steam show in the Valley of Ten Thousand Smokes, the creation of the monument was a kind of fraud. (In 1920, even before the decline was documented, economics-minded Alaska governor Thomas Riggs complained that "Katmai Monument serves no purpose and should be abolished.") To others looking back from today's much larger and ecologically rich park, the creation of the much smaller original monument, even if for bogus reasons, was fortuitous because it gave people time to realize just how many other things nearby deserved protection as well. And to me, it is yet another wonderful example of the serendipitous process by which the institution of the national park has evolved.

Parks routinely add new roles, or undergo significant realignment of the roles for which they were created. My book *Searching for Yellowstone* is largely an inquiry into how this process of "rediscovering" Yellowstone has made it such a dynamic and stimulating experiment in government stewardship of poorly understood resources. Many of the things for which we most treasure Yellowstone and other parks weren't even dreamed of by their founders. A national park is an organic institution, and much the better for its flexibility in the face of changing social values and growing ecological wisdom.

As it happened, there were questions about the durability of the geothermal activity in Katmai even during the deliberations that led to the creation of the monument. In 1918 the National Geographic Society sent a party of two men (again botanists—were there no unemployed geologists handy?) to make sure that the activity had not declined; they reported that it had not. And though I am surprised that the various bright people in the Interior Department and the Society should consider such a short-term evaluation as sufficient proof of stability in a geothermal system that was only six years old, I am not surprised, given the enthusiasm and fervor of the monument's boosters, that the report was good enough.

The difference between Yellowstone and Katmai was fundamental. Yellowstone's long, spectacular volcanic history is the result of a broad "hot spot" in the earth's crust—a plume of magma that came close to the surface of the earth under the entire region. The park's widespread hot spring and geyser basins, though each is much smaller than the Valley of Ten Thousand Smokes, are assured a perpetual supply of heat to simmer and evaporate groundwater that seeps into the various channels and systems of the geysers, hot springs, fumaroles, and mud pots. The Valley of Ten Thousand Smokes, on the other hand, was a temporary phenomenon. The heat generated by the initial 1912 volcanic activity was extreme, and is still more than enough to keep hot springs and steam vents in business near the volcanic cones themselves. But the broader scene, especially the ten- or twelve-mile-long ash flows of the main valley, lived off heat stored from the original days of the eruption, which allowed it to simmer groundwater quite impressively for a decade or two, but did not endure much beyond that. Even had the heat lasted or increased, the fragile, porous earth of the ash flows lacked the density and strength needed to support high-pressure geyser systems. The hope that the valley would generate geysers was forlorn and naive.

By the early 1930s, according to explorer-adventurer Father Bernard Hubbard, "a few feeble smokes" still rose from the upper end of the valley, and there was still some hydrothermal activity on the slopes and cones of some of the volcanic mountains, but the big show described by Griggs was all over. Hubbard (who is rightly regarded today as a heroic figure in Alaska history but sometimes comes across in his books and articles as pompously self-important) grumpily concluded that the valley was "a great disappointment. It is so inaccessible, so totally different from the enthusiastic descriptions of its first explorers, and finally, so belies the predictions of what might be expected of it, that it should be discontinued as a National Monument, and the trappers who formerly made an honest living in the Valley should be allowed to return there." It is unclear if by mentioning the "honest living" the trappers had formerly made there, Hubbard meant to contrast the dishonest living some were still making, even though the monument existed.

These dramatic changes in the valley fueled local resentment of the federal reservation, just adding to the frustration Alaskans felt over continued park service neglect of the place. But as national public interests and values changed, so did the park service's conception of the monument as a resource. By the time the park service finally established a staff presence in Katmai, at midcentury, there were stirrings of public realization that this was much more than a volcanic wonder. Eventually, by the 1960s, the tremendous expanse of wild land in Katmai National Monument, which underwent expansions of varying magnitudes in 1931, 1942, 1969, 1978, and 1980, was seen as valuable enough just for the sake of that wildness. Growing awareness of the wildlife and fisheries in all that wild land enhanced this view. The Valley of Ten Thousand Smokes is still a big attraction to visitors, but, as with Yellowstone's geysers, this original purpose for the reservation is now complemented by other roles that are as important, or even more important, in the eyes of a devoted public.

Even so, over the long haul of this century, there has been an odd symmetry in Wilson's 1918 proclamation. Its justifications of the monument as a scientific treasure and an inspiration for visitors seeking an understanding of volcanism are as valid as ever—Katmai's value as a scientific laboratory was not lessened by the stilling of the smokes. Like Yellowstone's geysers and hot springs, the fabulous steaming valley Griggs discovered was merely the surface expression of much greater and more durable forces, of considerably greater interest to science. The disappearance of the smokes and of the promise some saw in them now seems trivial, because the justification of Katmai as a replacement for a senescent Yellowstone was unnecessary all along. I doubt that many people shall ever feel badly about that.

Trundling along in the aging government Suburban, our much more modest expedition approached the valley from the opposite direction than Griggs had. At the end of the road, at Three Forks Overlook, there is a large cabin for visitors who need to dry, thaw out, or just have a quiet place out of the wind to eat lunch. The cabin stands on the edge of the last green rise before the valley. From it, you look up the valley across several miles of sand-colored ash deposits, one hundred to three hundred feet thick. Griggs's initial viewpoint from Katmai Pass is upward of twelve miles farther south, out of sight around the corner of a mountain. Without the distant mountains for perspective, it might not seem all that grand a sight, but with those peaks giving scale, and even without the smokes, the pale, flat expanse that rises slowly away from the base of the overlook, mile after uniform mile up the long valley to the very base of the mountains, is a startling and improbable landscape. From the height by the cabin, you have just enough elevation to make out some of the winding gorges that persistent local streams have cut back down through the ash to the old valley floor. The smokes may be dead, but the unlikely colors speak so clearly of warmth that you would not be surprised to see Griggs's columns of steam suddenly reappear.

We hiked the mile-and-a-half trail down to the floor of the valley so that we could get right up on the edge of the ash flows. Three streams—two from the ash-filled valley and one from the next valley over—join here to form the Ukak River, as brown and soupy a silt carrier as I've ever seen. It

looked like someone had taken some turbid midwestern river just at its peak of carrying off the topsoil of a thousand farms and tilted it into a steeper grade to give it an energy to match its mass.

Even with the streams, there is a desert mood to the big plain and its sheer, little canyons. The last stream to join, Knife Creek, emerges out of the bright ash flow from a canyon with all the slotlike characteristics of the scalloped gorges of the Colorado Plateau. There are big spires and knife-edged fins of ash along the stream, alternated with undulant surfaces more like dunes than walls. The yellow of the walls sometimes hints of pink, and for some strange reason seems to slump off into piles of gray. Scrubby vegetation is slowly colonizing some patches, and here and there, even on the most lunar flats, some plant or other is making a small living. At the end of the trail, Ukak Falls is a violent, unorganized chute of thick, muddy spray that drenches the nearby rock shelves and leaves tiny stone fragments, the shrapnel of erosion, scattered in the cracks and pockets well back from the water. As accustomed as I am to raw landscapes, it was kind of a relief to climb back up to the cabin through the comforting colors of the tundra lupines and geraniums. Even now, eighty years after the eruption and its hot rain of rock and dust, I have to agree that it's a Helluva job.

In 1901 Rex Beach, who later became a popular novelist, crossed Katmai Pass during an unsuccessful business venture, leaving one of the more lively descriptions of the country prior to the eruption. In his third novel, *The Silver Horde* (1909), he left a lurid, H. Rider Haggard-wannabe style description of the Katmai Pass portion of the Alaska range, "that desolate, skyscraping rampart which interposes itself between the hate of the Arctic seas and the tossing wilderness of the North Pacific. This range forms a giant, ice-armored tusk thrust out to the westward and curved like the horn of an African rhino, its tip pointed eight hundred miles toward the Asiatic coast, its soaring peaks veiled in perpetual mists and volcanic fumes, its slopes agleam with lonely ice fields. It is a saw-toothed ridge, for the most part narrow, unbroken, and cruel, and the rival winter gales roar over it in a never-ceasing war."

I don't mind admitting that I enjoy this overwrought kind of writing now and then, and even though it wasn't winter when we stood by the cabin before heading back for Brooks, the mountains did give us a modest display of just such a gale. The distant ash field a few miles to the south, toward the upper part of the valley, was busy with one of its frequent afternoon sandstorms, for good reason the subject of substantial local folklore, especially among hikers who have been caught in one. A long, upswept plume of smoky gray dust grew to blizzard proportions as we watched, engulfing several square miles in what must have been zero-visibility conditions. To be out there would be to risk a terrible sand-blasting. Most of the storm's dust cloud looked to be at least two hundred feet deep, and the high end in the front was five times that.

There is one more charming O. Henry twist in the saga of the creation and protection of Katmai as a national monument and then as a national park. In 1953 and 1954 G. H. Curtis of the University of California studied the ashfall depths at Mount Katmai and at Novarupta, a lower and much less visually dramatic volcanic vent six miles farther west. He decided, to the eventual agreement of the scientific community, that the main eruption, with its global effects and valley-long legacy of ash, had not occurred at Mount Katmai after all. More than forty years after the fact, it became clear that unobtrusive Novarupta was actually the main performer. I wonder, had Griggs and the leadership of the park service and the National Geographic Society known this, if they would have named the monument differently.

• • •

After dinner Marsha preferred to "stay home" for a little while, so I walked down the lakeshore to fish those wonderful rainbow riffles again at the head of the Brooks River. The fishing was a little slower, and my biggest fish was "only" eighteen inches.

In a spot like this, so new and ripe with almost unspeakable promise, my fishing sometimes degenerates into a lower form of recreation in which I remind myself of certain young wolves I have watched. These are the "teenagers," as much as a year old and looking full-size to the casual observer, but still fairly useless in the serious trade of being a wolf. I've watched packs scattered out as they moved along a low valley in northern Yellowstone, the alpha pair and various aunts and uncles all business and fully occupied with shopping for a promising elk, while these adolescents go kiting off across a meadow after large, healthy herds of hopelessly uncatchable ones. They easily succeed in getting the elk running, and though they are unable to catch any of them, and probably wouldn't have known what to do if they did get one within reach, they are so swept up in the thrill of the chase that they may run the herd for hundreds of yards. I can almost hear the "Yeeeeehaa!" that their overcharged young systems are expressing right then.

Fishing can be something like that if you let its excitement sweep you into the mindless rush of something better done with a little more thought. Recently in Yellowstone, a friend and I were about seventeen miles from the nearest road, along a stretch of stream that probably didn't get more than one fisherman per mile per month. In half an hour I landed at least ten beautiful wild cutthroat trout and lost as many more, mindlessly hurrying each fish from the hook (Yeeeeehaa!) just so I could hook another and see that reckless little attack of theirs (their Yeeeeehaa! right back at me) break the surface after the fly. It's not necessarily a bad way to fish, and it's an understandable response to the rare chance to have such generous fishing, but after a while my friend did chide me for my carelessly hasty handling of the fish as I discarded each one back into the water. The actual act of catching fish may not be all that serious an intellectual challenge, but it does have its own sense of respect, not only for the fish, but also for the experience. Rather like the ease of seeing bears at the falls, the catching of fish when there is no limit to their numbers requires a certain adjustment in our sense of proportion and our definition of what constitutes an accomplishment.

The Brooks River reminded me that fishing doesn't have to be fast or even successful for that mood to slip over me. I was so anxious to cover so many of these glorious, little aquatic targets that I rushed from one to another just as if I were catching something and having fun. If I had stuck with it a little longer and continued to catch fish at the same slow pace, it might even have been possible for me to be disappointed, there in Alaska. That was such a disturbing revelation that I quit.

There was a meeting that night in the auditorium building over by the cabins. Mark Wagner, creator of the brown bear booster program, decided to get as many people together as he could and talk about the problem with the photographers at the falls platform. Marsha and I thought this might be very interesting, partly because photographers present so many challenges to park managers everywhere, and maybe just a little because we could enjoy the luxury of not having to decide anything or take part in any unpleasant administrative actions. We sat in the back and kept quiet.

Few places reveal the dark underside of amateur photography as clearly as a famous natural attraction. In his *Rambles through an Alaskan Wild* (1979), certainly the most handsomely produced book I've found on Katmai, photographer Dave Bohn levels a pretty firm attack on his fellow nature photographers:

> The arrogance of people-photographers who invade privacy with the camera is, I think, a well-documented phenomenon. Less well considered is the matter of the wildlife photographer, who is just

as arrogant as the counterpart, or perhaps more so. More so because, with some exceptions, wildlife cannot strike back, whereas the person whose privacy has been tampered with can attempt to punch the invader in the nose and/or smash the camera.

Bohn's concern here was with the harassment of wildlife that routinely occurs in national parks and other public lands. Anywhere animals are to be found, people gather and crowd them and drive them from view by pushing in for just a little closer shot. But at Brooks Falls, the platform itself mostly controlled the extent to which the photographer could impinge on the animal's space. It didn't, however, prevent people from breaking park rules and vocally harassing the animals. Why does merely holding a camera make people clap, whistle, and otherwise interfere with the behavior of the animal just to get it to look at them? The pros didn't feel a need to do this. Why is a picture of an animal that you have obviously interrupted and made to look at you better than a picture of that same animal doing something natural?

What concerned Wagner was the social side of the same problem. Photographers are accustomed to be being crammed into small spaces together if the shot is worth it. But it was going to be up to the photographers to decide just how much impinging they had to do on each other's spaces.

I suppose about twenty people showed up, which struck me as a good crowd for such a small place with such a low visitation. Several were serious photographers. I recognized a couple that I'd seen manning the big industrial-strength tripods that week, and wondered how they'd take any criticism that Mark or others in the room might offer. I suffered a mild conditioned response to such public meetings over park issues, anticipating the possibility of anger and confrontation.

But Mark handled it very well, and it was, at least for the moment, a success. In a consistently nonthreatening manner, he pointed out the obvious: The big camera gear caused each photographer to occupy a disproportionate amount of space. On busy days, those tripods were interfering with the fair sharing of the platform. What could be done?

There were people there who shared his concern, but everyone was polite, and the photographers themselves had a great answer. They volunteered to switch over to smaller camera mounts, the kind that allow the camera to be clamped onto the platform's heavy wooden railing, an acceptably steady base for the biggest lens. The next day, and the day after that, the platform was a lot roomier.

Crossing the bridge on our way to and from the lodge area was now a process we embarked upon with more uncertainty. The sow that had showed up yesterday seemed to have settled on the bridge area as a good fishing site. There were few other bears around yet, anyway, so she could count on some peace and quiet here. Unwilling to risk her cub's life at the falls, she still wanted to fish, and had little trouble tolerating the human watchers and fishermen who were regularly shifted out of her way when she came through. It may also have been that all the human activity at the bridge kept the big males away; she may in effect have been using us as a shield.

For the rest of our visit, she was a fixture at the bridge. She was happy to settle down in the middle of it, youngster at her side, for an hour or so at a time, inadvertently backing up pedestrians at the platform and over where the path emerged from the woods on the other side of the river. She would plop her big, round bottom down, rest her chin almost pensively on the guard rail, and stare off into the trees. She would walk out to the end of one of the pontoons that extended several feet beyond the railing, then rise to her hind legs and give a little jump—a very human movement, like a small boy trying to dislodge another boy from the end of a diving board. Sometimes the pontoon's sudden surge up and down would spook a salmon or two out from under the bridge, and she'd do a spectacular belly-flop into the water to try to get it. Sometimes she would succeed, and rise sopping from the river with the fish in her mouth. The first time we saw her catch a salmon, it must have been her first of the day, because she wasn't even willing to share it with the cub. She brought it ashore at the far end of the bridge, where the impatient cub stood whining for it, then she fled from the cub, running the entire length of the bridge and past the platform, salmon in mouth, bawling cub in hot pursuit, looking for a quiet place to eat the fish in peace.

For watching bear behavior, Marsha and I soon decided that we preferred the bridge platform to the falls. There might be more, and bigger, bears lumbering around at the falls, and there was always the chance that you'd get to witness some major altercation between two of the river's real behemoths—the kind of fight that even makes headlines in Anchorage—but there's nothing like a mother bear with cub at heel for steady entertainment.

There is some confusion about the term "cub." Casually used, it means any young bear. Strictly speaking, it is best applied to any young-of-the-year, a bear just born that spring. But it is a lot less awkward to call any young bear a cub rather than deal with drier terms such as "juvenile" or, even less heartfelt, "subadult."

Generalizing the label of the little bears is also nice because it is hard to know exactly how old a young bear is. I have a pretty high level of confidence that I can recognize a cub born this year, but after that, even the best bear observers

I know admit that it gets a lot harder. A prosperous yearling may be larger than a runt two-year-old. Much confidence is expressed by many bear observers that they are looking at a one-, two-, or three-year-old bear. Some even extend their diagnoses to lone young bears no longer following their mothers, and announce that this is a four- or five-year-old. Unless it's a bear I've watched in successive years and have some reason to recognize the mother, I tend to call them all cubs and admit that I can't tell how old they are.

This sow's cub was pretty good-sized, and my best guess is that it was an advantaged two-year-old. It was a textbook cub in that it seemed to be pretty much a nuisance to her. There is evidence that females with only one cub form a different bond than if they have more than one; they tend to play more with a single cub than they would with two or three, for example. For all I know, the bridge female may have started with two or three—mortality is high among very young bears—but for whatever reason, this cub was now her only charge, and though she was as protective as she needed to be, there were times when she was just as glad to park the cub along the bank and go out in deep water.

She fished in other ways than from the bridge. She would stand on her hind legs, up almost to her chin in the deep, slow water downstream from the bridge; from our vantage point she was not moving. Apparently she just waited for a salmon to swim within reach, because one minute she would be just standing, and the next she would be standing chewing on a salmon that she had just lifted to her mouth. She would sometimes eat the fish right there; the sounds of popping bones were accompanied by the soft whines of her cub, which watched hungrily from the bank because he (I'm not sure why I decided it was a male cub; perhaps because it seemed so rude) did not want to swim out to her. One day, when Diver came snorkeling through on his rounds and scared her off for a while, he stood in the same place and caught fish the same way. They made it look so easy that I wondered why they didn't do it more often.

The river, which I waded so cautiously, was entirely her realm. Because of her cub, she was perhaps less mobile than a lone male would have been, but she crossed the river regularly, leaving the cub no choice but to wait or follow her. When she was obviously on the move to a new place, he always followed. As she waded through some deeper spot where we fishermen had stood moments before and would stand again moments later, the cub anxiously dog-paddled along behind her. When the water got deep, she stood up on her hind legs and walked like the rest of us.

Several times we watched her or Diver walking this way downstream and had a delightful shock of recognition. The push and lift of the current gave them a buoyant, loping gait exactly like an astronaut on the moon.

Okay Where You Are

Fishing the Brooks River is defined by anglers as "combat fishing."
> —National Park Service, *Bear Facts* (1998)

It was a damp, drizzly morning threatening worse, so while I stopped at the bridge to fish, Marsha continued on to the lodge and settled in to read in front of the grand, circular fireplace. Bill Allan was on the platform at the bridge, a comforting figure up there both because he knew a lot about bears (after four days here, Marsha was making dark remarks about not wanting to be a widow) and because he knew so much about the fish.

I waded in just upstream of the bridge and worked the wide, deep run there with various large trout flies, hoping for one of the famous lower-river rainbows. These flies, which imitate small fish, are fished with a lot of action, jerking and hurrying them across the current to trigger the predatory urges of the trout. (These are the same urges we seek not to trigger in dogs and bears when we advise each other not to run from them; it is said that running from a bear is rather like saying "fetch!")

But I quickly snagged a salmon, then another. Pulling a fly diagonally across the river like that guarantees that if there are salmon present, eventually the fly will drag across one's back and hang up on a fin. The second one was well hooked and put up a long fight before I could see that it was snagged in the back and just horsed it in as fast as I could to get it off the hook. Right away I hooked another that lunged heavily about halfway out of the water before throwing the hook. It finally dawned on me that all these hookups were nature's way of telling me I was fishing for the wrong species. I decided I might as well fish for salmon on purpose, so I put on one of Bill's little green mutants and began the slow ritual, casting slightly upstream, then, through a series of mends of the floating line, encouraging the fly to sink deep and drift directly downstream into the faces of salmon.

A tall, black-haired young man of about sixteen was fishing just downstream, about halfway between me and the bridge, when word reached us through distantly overheard conversations that a bear was coming. I called up to Bill for details, and he said that yes, there was a bear coming down the trail from the lodge, but it wasn't even to the bridge yet, so we should keep fishing. It might turn and go off down the lakeshore, or turn the other way back into the woods and head upstream.

It didn't. It came right on, and though I couldn't see it yet because I was low in the water, when it got to the north end of the bridge, perhaps sixty yards from me, Bill called down that we should take our lines out of the water.

The young man was not wading as deeply as I and was closer to the bridge, so I asked him, "Is it on the bridge?"

"Yeah," he said with considerable dismay. He was wearing rented waders and had no other gear but his rod. This was his first day.

The bear ambled slowly onto the bridge, and I could see it. From this short and decreasing distance, standing up to my navel in the river, I had the novel sensation of looking *up* at an approaching brown bear. This gave me an entirely different visual perspective and psychological stance than it had from up on the platforms.

I was also in the odd position of having more experience at Brooks than the person next to me, this young man who was now twenty feet closer to the bear than I was. He was getting vocal in his agitation. Mimicking Bill's calm professionalism as best I could, I suggested that we move upstream a little and out into deeper water. I knew that if this had actually been an attacking bear, the water depth would make no difference, but I reasoned that if we did need to make for the trees on the other shore, we might as well cross some of that deeper water now. I also felt a strong need to do something rather than just stand there watching a huge brown bear saunter past.

I am tall enough to wade into pretty deep water, and this teenager was about my height (though he lacked my ballast). Even at that, we were soon up to the tops of our waders in the slow-moving river. As I gripped the top of my waders to pull them as high as I could under my arms, my shirt cuffs were dragging in the water. I was on my tiptoes. When the bear arrived, I had already been standing in the cold water too long without a break and was starting to shiver. So as the bear dawdled on the bridge, I suggested that we might as well go on across the rest of the deep water and get out on the other side of the river. Maybe if we got to that side before the bear did, we could move upstream more easily and put some distance between him and us.

But as we started that way, Bill, his words echoed by a female voice that had more concern in it, told us to stay where we were because another bear, one we couldn't see because of the intervening tall grass, had just come out of the trees upstream of us and seemed to be heading our way. The woman tourist up on the platform with Bill thought it was important to emphasize to us that this second bear was darker. Learning we were being approached by a bear we couldn't even see was somehow more disturbing than watching the one on the bridge. Thank heavens for that woman, though—at least we knew it was darker.

We were now between two bears, a situation that happens routinely here once the salmon run really gets going and three or four dozen bears are fishing. I had seen such a standoff already, from a distance. I was walking down the trail by the lodge when I noticed a group of six or eight visitors standing in a clearing, all aiming their binoculars at the Cutbank, just past the second bend upstream from the bridge. Three fishermen, standing back-to-back and facing outward like musketeers making a last stand, were between two large brown bears, both of which were just crouched in the grass watching them. It was a still life with tension, and it went on as long as I watched. For all I know they're all still standing there, trying to figure out who should go where.

Our closest bear stopped to sniff the side of the bridge near one of the pontoons, a place that was of great interest to all the bears. I was told by a lodge employee that when the bridge was assembled, some salmon had somehow gotten trapped in a float compartment, or wedged in between sections of the bridge, or in some other way had permanently left a powerful scent there. This spot never failed to get an inspection from a passing bear, leaning through the rail and nosing the side of the bridge for a good snort of whatever essence remained.

Neither the teenager nor I was comfortable with just waiting, and I suppose our restlessness must have been visible, because Bill called down to us, "You're okay where you are."

Under his breath, but clearly for my edification as well as his own, the teenager replied, "Yeah, asshole, you're up there where it's safe."

It concerned me that if the bear on the bridge continued across, it might meet the darker bear, which was apparently coming down the riverbank toward the other end of the bridge. One of them might bounce off this encounter in our direction. But when the bear finally did get across the bridge, it went the other way, toward the lake. The darker bear left, too. We never did get to see it.

Bill called down, "You can go back to fishing."

And I called back, "Can we leave?" People on the platform laughed.

Two weeks after we left, Dr. Christopher Servheen visited Brooks Camp. For the past two decades or so, Chris, whom I knew slightly because the bear world is a small one, has been one of the leading voices in grizzly bear conservation, in good part because he is grizzly bear recovery coordinator for the U.S. Fish and Wildlife Service. In that role, he has abundant opportunities to get nationally crosswise of all parties in the endless debates over land management, and he has never been reluctant to do so when his professional opinion required it.

Bob Barbee invited Chris to visit Brooks and look the situation over, then give him a report. Chris was accompanied by bear biologist John Schoen of the Alaska office of the National Audubon Society, and their report was a ringing endorsement of the less well-articulated alarm that Marsha and I had felt all week. My rather muddled emotional responses to repeated close encounters with bears had not led me to formulate anywhere near this concise and urgent a statement:

> In our professional opinion, the situation at Brooks River will eventually lead to [a] serious bear-human encounter resulting in the death or serious injury of one or more visitors. The human use of the Brooks River area, the placement of the facilities, and the high density of bears make this site the most dangerous bear-human encounter situation we have ever seen. This is a very serious matter. The reason for this is the constant interaction between large numbers of bears and uninformed visitors along the trails leading to the viewing platforms, and within the existing facilities along Naknek Lake shore. The issue is not if a death or injury will result, it is when it will happen. Such a death or serious human injury from a bear at Brooks River will forever change the complexion of how visitors use the area, how the facility will be managed, and how people both at the site and in general will view bears. This incident will erode public support for bears and will result in a negative view of the NPS [National Park Service] and the concession operation. The time to act is now before this death or serious injury occurs.

Servheen and Schoen supported and even expanded on existing park service proposals for relocating all the facilities well back from the river corridor. They suggested closing the falls viewing platform during the darker evening and morning hours so that the more shy bears, the ones reluctant to come so close to humans, could have a turn there. They pointed out that besides bears becoming habituated to people, "humans also habituate to bears at Brooks," meaning that over time people become more and more willing to have bears closer and closer. The longer the period during which nobody gets hurt, the more comfortable the people get at close quarters.

Judging from some of the human behavior I saw at Brooks, and from what I've read in the public dialogue that the park's development concept plan for Brooks generated, there are plenty of people who regard the bears as nearly harmless, and they can point to what seems to be an extraordinary safety record to "prove" it. Unlike the other major grizzly bear national parks, no one has ever been killed by a bear at Brooks. There are hardly even any records of injuries. Many years go by between occasions when bears and humans actually make contact.

The most serious injury occurred in July 1966. The victim was a camper named John Huckabee, who many years later was kind enough to provide the park service with a full description of his experience. As he landed on the beach at Brooks, he told a concessioner employee that he "wanted to photograph brown bears, to which he replied that I '—would be lucky to see a bear.' I consider this comment, foolishly made and more foolishly taken, as the main factor in the subsequent attack." Huckabee, who said he was experienced at camping in bear country in Alaska and around Yellowstone, assumed there were no bears nearby and so was not careful with his camping arrangements. He set up camp not far from another camper, and settled in:

Before dark, I caught a lake trout for dinner. It was too large for one [person], so quite a bit was left over. I simply placed the remains on a rock. I did not wash the skillet, but left it by the fire, ready for breakfast. All food was left on the ground in the vicinity.

I then went to sleep about 10 meters from the fire place. I was awakened, during complete darkness, by the sounds of the bear rummaging about, knocking over dishes and equipment. I looked at it for a moment, and it did not appear to see me. I decided it was too close to run, so I elected to lay low. After a few minutes, it walked over towards where I lay. I remember the audible soft thud of its footsteps. I was on my abdomen, and the bear began to sniff my sleeping bag. It rather delicately hooked under my hip with foreclaws and rolled me over. I decided that a bite on the backside was better than a bite in the abdomen, so I rolled back over and forthwith received the bite on the backside. I yelled as loud as I could, and my impression was that the animal was startled. I do not recall—never did—any details while I was in the thing's teeth. It dropped me about 3-4 meters away. I remained motionless and quiet, and it did not bother me any more, but continued ransacking my camp. Sometime later the other camper walked up, properly making lots of racket. The bear left like a shadow, without a sound. I called out to the camper to help and beware. He satisfied himself that the animal was gone (he never saw it) and then assisted me to the HQ [headquarters] area.

Huckabee was given first aid and flown out for hospitalization. By that fall, the bite wounds had healed, but "by far the worst post-attack phenomenon was the nightmares, which deprived me of sleep for two to three weeks, but which did not disappear entirely for almost ten years." As to the matter of who was to blame, he never considered a lawsuit, "because I felt the responsibility was my own." This admirable wisdom and restraint on his part is in the official record, but the story seems to have become somewhat muddled in successive informal tellings. By the time we visited Brooks, thirty-two years later, it was at least a minor part of local folklore that Mr. Huckabee had not survived the attack. A somewhat stylized version of the tale has evolved over the years, in which some man fell asleep on a trail and was killed by a passing bear.

The official report of that year's bear incidents also mentioned that "one other person was stepped on as he slept in the campground and a young boy was apparently touched by a bear in the process of stealing a fish from him at the old fish cleaning table."

In 1991 park ranger Linda Marr was walking to the falls platform when she encountered an aggressive bear. Marr had been making noise and was almost to the platform when, coming around a bend in the trail (the report seems to be talking about Scary Hill), she saw the bear, reported as being a "medium-sized sow" that had bluff-charged several other parties. When the bear charged Marr, she got behind a tree, but in grabbing the tree, her arm was wrapped around the trunk in the bear's view, and the bear bit her arm before leaving. The wound was not serious, and after treatment in King Salmon, she was back at work the next day.

It is impossible to know how many close encounters there have been at Brooks over the years. For some periods, the reporting system dealt only with more serious events. In the period 1965 to 1981, for example, when bears and people were both less abundant at Brooks, 113 "incidents" were known to have occurred. These included thirty-six break-ins of buildings, eighteen property-damage cases in the campground, twelve occasions where bears got food left loose on the lakeshore or in boats and planes, eight times that bears found garbage in the campground, eight cases of bears damaging fishing tackle at the river, two bears charging a fisherman with a fish, and one episode described as a "garbage dump incident." The very existence of a garbage dump suggests the magnitude of the problem.

But even in more recent years, when a conscientious effort has been made to record close encounters, it seems clear that all the people wandering around unattended must have often met with bears and not said anything about it, if indeed they realized it was something worth reporting. In 1991, the year of Marr's injury, there were a reported 115 incidents in which people approached to less than the fifty-yard distance recommended as the minimum safe distance from adult bears, or one hundred yards from females with young. There were seventeen reported cases of bluff charges, although it was not known how many bears were involved.

Marsha and I followed an older couple down the trail one day near the lodge. They walked meekly along about ten yards in front of us, visibly flinching when we clapped our hands or yelled. Not only did they not make such noises, they were obviously bothered by them. By any practical definition, they were sneaking along, but they were trying to enjoy a beautiful place, something we were making more difficult for them with our noise. As we watched visitors from various countries move around Brooks, we wondered how many of these people had actual cultural barriers between them and the prescribed behavior. It has always bothered me to have to make noise in such lovely surroundings as bear country provides, even though I knew it was necessary. People coming from a country that either never had wild brown bears or lost them hundreds of years ago have no meaningful tradition of caution to apply to such a situation. This doesn't forgive them, or excuse them from risk, but it does argue for aggressive supervision of their activities.

But the baffling fact remains that for all the inattention of the visitors, and all the close calls, there are almost no human injuries. The two I mentioned are perhaps the most serious in more than thirty years. Even though I agree with Servheen and Schoen's assessment of the danger, I still wonder at this amazing shortage of actual physical harm done by so many wild bears to so many uncontrolled people. There is an aura here that I cannot comprehend, like an enchantment or charm laid on by higher forces that keeps the blood inside the people against all odds.

But neither can I relax. There are more bears and more people all the time. In a few days of casual observation, I saw shocking casualness in the faces of visitors, especially fishermen, who appeared to be taking the enchantment for granted, if they even recognized it at all. Simple lack of attention by people who had formed no personal stance one way or the other about the bears was just as common, and almost as alarming.

Elsewhere I have argued that it is important that there be risk in the wilderness experience; that without treacherous stream crossings, unpredictable weather, wild animals, and all the other unruly features of wild nature, something essential is lost. A defanged, neutered, manicured landscape may be beautiful, but it is not wilderness. The concern that Servheen, Schoen, and many of us have at Brooks is not that wildness or danger are somehow wrong. In the vast reaches of Katmai's millions of acres, we would not dream of suggesting any moderation of nature's effects. But at Brooks, a different set of rules seem to apply. Many of the people arriving there daily are, like my mother, fresh off the tour boat and unprepared for anything resembling a wilderness experience. They are thrust into extraordinarily close contact with wilderness risks for which they have not been prepared. Unlike the hiker who chooses to participate in the wilderness's riskier environment, these visitors have not been asked to make such a choice. They are sightseers and flightseers, and tomorrow they'll be back in the buffet line on their cruise ship, or cruising the knickknack shops in Anchorage, or taking in a movie in Fairbanks. Great arguments could be held over whether places like Brooks make it too easy for these people—if there shouldn't be a little more earning involved to witness such a grand wild spectacle—but for now managers do not have the luxury of pondering such questions. The salmon show up, the bears show up, and the people show up, and somehow it all has to remain peaceful.

By comparison with the bear-safety educational program of every other park I've visited, Katmai's, with its required orientation, its bear booster program, and its focused bear-viewing areas, is exceptionally intensive. But as Servheen and Schoen point out, no management program can concurrently offer so much individual discretion to visitors and at the same time guarantee their safety. The managers themselves have been saying that for years. From a statistical point of view, it is almost as if the park's visitors are doing all they can to tempt fate and send the odds over the top, into the certainty that Servheen and Schoen say is awaiting us.

But let me tell you how I think it will go. Speaking as a nonprofessional whose opinion is not weighty like theirs, but as a historian who has studied park issues like this as they have progressed over the last century or so, I think that Servheen and Schoen are right in their prediction that someone is going to get hurt by a bear. I also think that it will take the tragedy of a human death—as opposed to a human injury—to fully activate the various consequences that Servheen and Schoen predict for the bears and the park in the aftermath of such a tragedy. Past injuries have not done it, and they have rarely made a difference in any other park. Only a death can do it.

I also think that the tragedy will not change a lot of minds. When a bear finally kills someone, whatever changes it may or may not force on management, it's not going to cause much of a shift in the opinion spectrum among people already familiar with Brooks. Those of us who think that the place is a little crazy can smugly say, "See? See?! We tried to tell you so!" But the people who don't believe that there is a serious problem here can be almost as smug. They can point out that even now that this first death has happened—"after all these years!"—Brooks still has one of the best safety records of all the parks. What does one killing mean? We shot the bear, didn't we? Doesn't that solve the problem? The exception proves the rule!

The first time a bear kills someone at Brooks might be a lot like the first time a bear killed someone in Yellowstone. In 1915 a bear dragged a member of a road maintenance crew from his camp in the middle of the night and killed him. The whole episode was seen as such an aberration of bear behavior that even leading bear "authorities" (there were virtually no actual bear scientists then, just some men who spent a lot of time in bear country) were amazed at this unusual behavior. They saw it as a freak occurrence rather than a bear doing what bears sometimes do. Nobody learned anything, because they thought there was nothing to learn. They killed the bear by luring it in with food until it stood over a charge of dynamite, then blasting it.

This alternative view will not help the dead person (or the bear, for that matter). It certainly won't shield the National Park Service from the wrongful death tort claim that will probably be filed by the victim's family (no one will sue the people who resisted changing the layout of the facilities). But it stands a strong chance of weakening the public will to do things differently at Brooks.

In 1967, when two young women were killed in separate bear attacks in one night in Glacier National Park, the furor was enormous, and it did eventually have some effects on bear management. And, as Servheen and Schoen predict for Brooks, it was harmful to the public image of wild grizzly bears. There were even calls for exterminating all grizzly bears in Yellowstone and Glacier. But the amazing coincidence of dual deaths in Glacier, involving separate parties of humans and separate bears in different parts of the park, made for a sensationally bizarre story—so much so that it was celebrated in a book, *Night of the Grizzlies*—and it happened in a heavily traveled national park that everyone had heard of. Odds are good that when news of Brooks's first human fatality reaches the outside world, the media will give us a short note about someone being killed by a bear in the great undifferentiated wilds of Alaska, and the world will wonder, "So what's new?"

One thing that could change this is if someone has a video camera running right then. All at once, the remote wilds of Alaska will be transformed into evening television, and it is impossible to predict what the consequences might be for the National Park Service, or the public, or the bears.

The puzzle for me when I consider this eventuality is that even with things as they are at Brooks right now, if I were not a blissfully married man with many other things to do, I would try to find a way to live and work there at least one whole season. All it would take would be for Marsha to suddenly wise up and boot me out, and I would be looking for application forms. The power of Brooks is so seductive, and has so many wonderful elements including the bears, that it would be irresistible despite the danger. The charm, or enchantment, or delicate detente, or whatever it is that keeps this place going has reached me right over the top of my better judgment. If they would have me, I would go.

Perhaps, in some convoluted way, my willingness to participate reveals the durability of the conviction that it's okay to keep Brooks the way it is. Perhaps, in some convoluted way, that makes some sense of its own—Brooks is so important for so many reasons that the risk to human life seems trivial. But I doubt it. Long ago, in Yellowstone's last open garbage dump, I had grizzly bears walk right past my car door, within easy reach. In Glacier, I've walked for miles in cover so dense that a face-to-muzzle confrontation could have occurred at any time. But never in my waking hours have I imagined a place like this, where peril has been given such an innocent and beautiful face, and where the connection with wildness at its most explosive is so casually had. No wonder people can't get over it, and no wonder it is so hard to change.

• • •

In Jean Bodeau's helpful guidebook, *Katmai National Park and Preserve, Alaska* (1996), there is a big picture of Tom Ferguson, one of our hosts, holding a rainbow trout considerably larger than any I caught while at Brooks. Tom, like Bill Allan, is a veteran Katmai fisherman, and he told me one of the most intellectually stimulating fishing stories I have heard in years. He said that he often catches the sockeyes on a bare hook. Using exactly the techniques the other fly fishermen use, he simply puts a hook on the leader instead of a real fly. He makes the same casts, and lets the hook drift through the school of fish just as he would a fly. He catches about as many fish that way as he does with a fly. I assume that other Alaskan fishermen have made this same discovery.

Tom was not suggesting that sockeyes are as likely to eat a bare hook as they are to eat some gaudy fluorescent concoction that a fly tier labored over so hopefully. This was not like the satisfying stunt of catching a naive backcountry trout on a bare hook; all you need to do that is a pondful of naive fish, such as are common in any western wilderness area, and a little patience. Cast a small bare hook out and retrieve it slowly until some little fish mistakes it for something alive; maybe it actually looks like a little worm or leech, twisting through the water.

But that's not what Tom was saying. He pointed out that when he landed a sockeye on a bare hook, it was usually hooked in a specific way: The hook was firmly embedded in the hinge of the jaw, on the outside of the fish's "lip," on the side opposite from where Tom was standing when he cast.

He figured that it happened like this. As the long line and leader drifted along, crosswise of the stream, cast after cast, it passed through the school of salmon again and again.

Eventually, one of these drifts put the line itself into the slightly open mouth of a salmon, where it easily slid up against the back of the jaw. As the rest of the line between the fish and Tom continued to drift with the current, it pulled the line sideways across the open mouth of the salmon until the hook hung up on the outside of the hinge of the fish's jaw.

This small revelation asks big questions about the nature of sport. The first premise of sportfishing is that the angler must fool the fish into taking a bait, lure, or fly that contains a hook. The goal is to trick the fish into making a mistake. It is this fundamental premise that compels us to regard any fish hooked elsewhere than in its mouth as "foul-hooked" and thus not acceptable. Snagging fish, though it is legally practiced as a type of sport in a few places in North America, is generally regarded as beneath the dignity of serious sportsmen. At Brooks, foul-hooked fish must be released immediately.

But Tom's salmon, though hooked in the mouth—or, more accurately, just on the outside of the lip and therefore on the vague edge of most definitions of "fair-hooked"—did not participate in the traditional definition. The salmon was not fooled into taking the hook. The salmon involuntarily became fair-hooked. It was snagged in the mouth.

Sport is highly mutable. It changes over time, and its ethical framework is almost always dependent upon local circumstances. I suspect that if you asked a number of the more thoughtful Alaskan sportsmen if they considered snagging salmon in the mouth ethical, they would say that it depends on the salmon. If that is the only way to get a reliable hookup, if it isn't too easy to do (it does take most of us a lot of casts per hookup), and if it requires certain minimum skills, then they would probably say that it's okay. The most thoughtful would probably also make their approval conditional, depending upon the well-being of the salmon population—if catching fish this way did no harm to the natural resource, then it would be okay. I also suspect that if you asked the great number of less inquiring fishermen the same question, they wouldn't consider it worth bothering with. It was fair-hooked, wasn't it? I was legal, wasn't I? What's the big deal?

The big deal is subtle. As I and other fishermen demonstrated at Brooks, the excitement felt when hooking a salmon is largely a reflexive act itself. For me, at least, that first surge of power against the rod, arms, and back—that first instant of taking effect—is angling's premier moment, when connection and success are most deeply felt, and hope is most fully realized. I am sure that countless fishermen have excitedly played such a fish, then suffered retroactive disappointment upon discovering that it was foul-hooked. (With enough experience, however, one develops a sense, a feel, about how a fish fights that raises a vague suspicion that something is wrong well before the fish can be seen to be foul-hooked.)

But disapproval of snagging fish is a cultural response. Through training, the fisherman comes to respect the ethical code that rejects snagging—simpler urges are suppressed and replaced by what is hoped to be a higher view. In this complex an intellectual and emotional enterprise, the angler will consciously quiet the thrill of that initial contact until the fish is seen to be fair-hooked. The first sight of the taut fly line tracing a course straight as the flight of Dinesen's bullet to the mouth of the fish is almost as great a relief as is finally getting the fish to hand.

Because we have defined the sport in certain ways, and given success such constraints, we have to wait before we can

enjoy the hookup. If we have not fully earned the fish's engagement in this process, something is diminished in our sense of a difficult thing done right. We wonder if we cheated.

Alaska's sportfishing regulations appear unequivocal on this: "It is unlawful to intentionally snag or attempt to snag any fish in fresh water. 'Snag' means hook a fish elsewhere than in its mouth. A fish unintentionally snagged elsewhere than its mouth must be released immediately." On the other hand, I have heard that in some locations, local practice allows some leeway, such as defining "fair-hooked" as including being hooked on the head somewhere near the mouth. Perhaps there is a feeling that if it's hooked close to the mouth, it probably was trying to get the fly or lure anyway, and just missed. I'm not convinced, but if I applied that rule to my Alaskan salmon-fishing experience, I would at least triple the number of "fair-hooked" fish I landed.

The matter returns us to the personalities of these salmon, as well. They may not be feeding, but they will some-times strike. Salmon may simply make a reflexive grab at something going by. They may be exercising the defensive mechanisms they will need once they build their spawning beds and must drive other fish away, including very small fish that are hoping to eat their eggs. While at Brooks, I am sure that I saw sockeye turn or snap at a fly as it passed, and those individuals could have been fair-hooked in the traditional sense of the word. There is a spectrum of opinion and behavior among the fish themselves.

Concern for such subtleties will always be too much of a bother for many sportsmen, for whom it is enough to honor the superficial definitions of the sport. To me, such ponderings are a necessary part of the sport. To many others, they're just self-indulgent intellectualizing, a lot of irrelevant navel gazing that interferes with the mood or distracts from the serious business of catching more fish.

A few weeks after leaving Brooks, I unexpectedly encountered some wonderful fishing for chum salmon in a small stream near Juneau. My unerring focus on the average revealed that these were typically thirty-inch fish, much stronger and heavier than the sockeyes, but about as unwilling to eat a fly. I am sure that I snagged a dozen or more for every one that I fair-hooked, though this was partly the result of there being more of them, packed more tightly together. They wallowed and rolled in the tidewater stream and well out into its estuary, galumphing through the shallows in a manner more porcine than piscine. As I stood there giddily casting over this biological tide of creatures, it seemed to me that with such great numbers of fish, my odds of attracting the attention of the few that might be eager to strike were very good. I am reasonably sure that I did catch some genuine strikers, fish that purposely took the fly. (They were hooked inside the mouth, well beyond my ability for precision casting.) There was a man at this stream who, like Jake at Brooks, had an uncanny gift for fair-hooking lots of fish, and, as with Jake, his success raised the unanswerable question of whether he was just better at snagging them in the mouth or somehow fished his fly so much better that the fish were more inclined to take it. Or whether he had a secret fly pattern. . . . Fishermen are hopeless dreamers, and never entirely give up on the idea that there really is a magically right way to do this, if only we could discover it.

So this matter has as much to do with the imponderable variations in individual fish behavior as it has to do with our cultural acts. We cannot decide absolutely about this element of sport without reference to the behavior of the sport's quarry, and that behavior is neither consistent nor adequately understood.

After a few hours of fishing for the chums, I spent a few minutes at another Juneau-area stream fishing for pink salmon, inelegantly known as "humpies" for their high back ridge. These smaller, fifteen- to twenty-inch fish, perhaps because they spend less time in salt water and do not lose their stream-feeding urges so completely, were eager feeders, coming several feet from their holding lies to attack the fly. No precision of placement of the cast was required of me. Should some quixotic soul ever decide that it was time to develop a formal ethical framework for dealing with issues like mouth-snagging, the resultant sporting code would have to vary to accommodate the idiosyncracies of the different species.

I don't expect such a code to arise. I assume that practically everyone in Alaska, like most people elsewhere, find their local fishing regulations and customs more or less satisfactory. But there is something going on here that demands our attention. Thinking about our behavior is as important a part of the challenge of fly-fishing as is thinking about fly pattern theory or presentation. Whenever we drift out onto these ethical fringes, we owe it to ourselves and our quarry to question what we're doing. The advantage that sport has over life is that we get to decide how to make it fair. Fishing would be a lot less fun if it didn't involve me in such mysteries and quandaries. In fact, I'm not sure I'd bother.

Late in the afternoon I fished again, just downstream of the footbridge. There were four or five of us fishing, taking turns at the best spot and moving up and down the bank almost as restlessly as the small cloud of salmon was oozing this way and that in the current. We had to stop sometimes because bears came by, but that gave us a chance to stand on the platform, which provided a much better view of the river and its fish. From the steeper, higher angle of the platform, we could see upward of a hundred salmon in a loose ellipse that contracted and expanded like a flock of birds wheeling over a meadow. After some of them passed under the footbridge and held in the current just above it, we noticed that there was a king salmon among the sockeyes, a much larger fish, like an aircraft carrier with its cruiser escort, that drew groans of admiration and covetousness from us. It moved up out of sight in deeper water before the bear let us return to fishing.

There was lots of action. I fair-hooked two and landed one. The whole time I was playing it, someone on the platform was giving us a running commentary on the bear that was just upstream of the bridge. The bear kept its distance, and I finally eased the fish into the shallows, where I could clearly see the line pointing toward its mouth and tell that it was fair-hooked. I hurriedly dragged the fish out onto the shore and leaned over to admire it. The fly was lightly attached to the outside of the opposite side of the jaw hinge, and after a second or two it came loose and fell out on the ground.

By then the bear had moved over into the lodge area, where it hung around the fish-freezing shed, right by the main trail from the lodge to the river. A little later we heard a few shots. A ranger fired "cracker shells," loud, explosive rounds, in the direction of the bear to scare it away and clear a path for the people, and the latest episode in the perennial skirmish between bears and people at Brooks was safely concluded.

The View
from Dumpling

*The idealism in the park concept has made every
American visiting the national parks feel just a little more
worthy. Our generosity to all creatures in the national
parks, this reverence for life, is a basic tradition,
fundamental to the survival of park idealism.*
 —Adolph Murie, *The Grizzlies of Mount McKinley*
(1981)

Late in the morning we hiked the first mile and a half
 of the trail up Dumpling Mountain, a twenty-four-
hundred-foot eminence a few miles northwest of Brooks
Camp. On the way, I felt like I was walking on the west side
of Glacier National Park, or along the Pacific coast's forested
trails. The tall, wet grasses, the geraniums, cow parsnip, fire-
weed, and other familiar plants, the damp overcast day, and
the edgy sensation of not being far from the nearest large
wild mammal were all familiar. On a grassy switchback, we
missed a turn and followed what I think was a moose trail for
several hundred yards into a pretty birch forest until the track
faded, then retraced our steps until we found the slightly

more distinct real trail. At the first rocky outcrop with a clear view of the river and the two lakes, we stopped to eat a little lunch and admire the view.

Directly below our outcrop, the slope we had just climbed and the bottomland on the north side of the river were a patchy mix of plant communities—several distinct shades of green that turn into many shades if you looked at them hard enough. Here and there, a few dark streaks of spruce stands alternated with patches of lighter willows, cottonwoods, alders, birches, and small meadows and marshy spots along the river. Just back from the north side of the river, along the shore of Naknek Lake, a few brown roofs poked up through the green to show the lodge complex. Our little house and the other buildings over along the shore of Brooks Lake might not have existed, for all we could see of them.

The river undulated its way in a north-trending semicircle across the isthmus from Brooks Lake to Naknek Lake. Even from this height, some short reaches of the river where it bends back on itself were obscured by streamside trees. The falls were not visible because at that point the river was

moving away from our viewpoint, but with small binoculars, we could see a bear or two moving around on what we judged to be the edge.

The far, or south, side of the river was almost solid spruce forest. The visual effect from an elevation of about a thousand feet and a distance of two miles was of a solid dark, shrubby-looking mat that commenced just back from the riverbank and extended uniformly for miles, out to the south along both lakeshores and on toward the Valley of Ten Thousand Smokes.

Standing back from the river like this, it is easy to imagine an only slightly different scene. In the four thousand or so years since dropping water levels allowed the formation of the isthmus across which the river now flows, people have been busy here. Pick a midsummer date during that period—let's say two thousand years ago—and look from this same eminence, and you might have seen even more signs of human activity: perhaps a *barabara* (pit house), or a small village of them, visible on the lowlands on either side of the river; smoke rising from fireplaces on Scary Hill (though I don't suppose they called it that); racks hung with long strips of drying salmon or moose meat. Some forested areas might have been cleared for one reason or another. Watercraft might have been visible, pulled onto the beach near the mouth of the river, or out on the open lake. There would have been less noise than now—no airplane or boat motors, no generators or buses. The landscape seems only gently haunted.

The rise of an awareness of cultural resources as a part of the "wild" landscape has begun to have a powerful effect on land-management agencies such as the National Park Service. This effect is not limited to what the professional managers are obliged to care for. It includes a rapidly changing appreciation of how culture and nature—and some people resist even considering them separate things—interacted in North America prior to the arrival of Europeans.

Fire ecologists were probably the first to insist that we reconsider the old Edenic notion of pre-Columbian North America as a perfect, unsullied wilderness where humans had no effects. They were certainly the first to forcefully and persuasively point out at least one way in which native people, rather than merely sitting on top of North American ecology and innocently consuming the odd berry or deer, were determined land managers. Though the jury is still out on many particulars, it is now clear that in many vegetation types, Native Americans set fires for a variety of reasons: to enhance the growth of favored plants in order to attract game or for harvest, to clear the land, to wage war, and of course, just like us, because they weren't paying attention and a campfire got away from them. Plant succession, wildlife habitat, and many subtle related features of the landscape's life were influenced by these activities.

But in the past thirty years, a host of other effects have been proposed and are still argued over. Practitioners of archaeology, anthropology, ecological history, dendrochronology, paleolimnology, and other specialized disciplines have applied finer and finer analyses to the role native people played in North America. They have started a scholarly and public conversation about the North American landscape that, though it promises to be contentious, is forcing us to a new understanding not only of native people, but also of the very idea of wilderness itself. There is widespread support for the belief that besides their use of fire, Native Americans influenced their environment in many other ways, including agricultural practices and the harvest of wildlife on land and in the water.

I wonder now how we ever could have thought otherwise. One thousand years ago in the Mississippi bottomlands across from present-day St. Louis, there was a city with a population about the same size as the London of that day, and from what I've read of the archaeology and anthropology, it sounds to me to have been at least as pleasant a place to live. An ancient American town of even one thousand inhabitants would place the same basic demands on its surroundings for water, fuel, sewage disposal, cultivable land, and food as a town of similar size might today, year after year, decade after decade, into the centuries. How could the several million Native Americans living in North America prior to the arrival of Columbus have avoided having some significant effects on the land they occupied?

Katmai National Park, though it might seem remote from the mainstream of the wilderness debate, has had wilderness values as a primary justification for nearly half a century, so it is inevitable that it be considered in this reshaping of our historical consciousness. In 1993 Ted Birkedal, chief of the Division of Cultural Resources for the Alaska Region of the National Park Service, published a paper in which he applied the newer thinking on Native American influences on their environment to some Alaskan areas. Birkedal pointed out that "with the exception of a possible, but unconfirmed, hiatus during part of the first millennium B.C., all available evidence attests to an intense and continuous occupation of the river margins by native Alaskans that extends well into the historic period."

The relationship that these people had with bears was no doubt complex, certainly involving spiritual attachments, to say nothing of an adversarial tolerance on some occasions and outright hostility at other times. Birkedal's admittedly preliminary investigation of studies of prehistoric bear-human relationships in Alaska suggested to him that it was highly unlikely that the people using Brooks River would have been willing to put up with dense concentrations of brown bears crowding into the river to catch the salmon that the people also wanted. Such an arrangement, in which human families were catching and drying large numbers of salmon right by the water, would have been even more dangerous than today's situation.

These people may not have had modern weapons, but they were by no means at the mercy of the big bears. They had effective techniques for killing bears, and prized bears for several reasons, including their meat. (In an 1887 survey of the Yukon River, Warburton Pike reported that when bears begin to feed on salmon, "the fishy taste is noticeable in their flesh almost immediately.") Like all people who share their environment with bears, these Alaskans had developed a rich tradition and lore surrounding the bears, but they did not regard them as an unapproachable enemy.

In the 1700s, when Russian fur traders began cruising the Alaskan coast in search of sea-otter pelts and other treasures, the native people experienced the first of a succession of intercultural jolts that dramatically changed their habits, their movements, their use of the land, and even their numbers, especially after smallpox and other European diseases arrived. Their use of places like Brooks had not been stable prior to the arrival of Europeans; as in the rest of North America, groups and tribes moved about; displaced, absorbed, or warred with one another; and experienced the gradual evolution of their own culture as the centuries passed. Indeed, archaeological evidence suggests that the Katmai area has undergone several such changes in the past few thousand years. But once whites arrived and exercised their own set of prerogatives, often doing so quite brutally, enslaving and relocating entire villages at a time, native life changed at a faster pace and to a greater extent.

One of the side effects of this great human tragedy is that we now have little way of knowing the specifics of local ecological conditions prior to their alteration by European influences. There is no indication that Russians ever visited Brooks, but their effects would have been felt there. Native people dragooned into the servitude of the fur traders were people whose effects on native animals were drastically changed. As the native people adjusted to the new economic regime, their hunting practices adjusted to the market. All of this occurred well before scientific surveys and exploring parties gave us written records of most of Alaska. Thus in the case of Brooks River, there can be no written accounts of what the scene looked like when the area was unaffected by whites, and thus are we hard pressed to say what is "natural" there. Human activities were not constant there for the thousands of years before whites arrived, and after whites reached the region, those activities changed even faster.

In 1940 biologist Victor Cahalane found a "crude frame for a one-man boat which was lying among the willows near the outlet of Brooks River." He asked a local native man about it:

> According to him, a hunter would walk up the Savonoski River [another stream flowing into Naknek Lake east of Brooks River, well known for its concentrations of bears during salmon runs] until he succeeded in shooting a bear. He would then make a boat frame from alders that he would cut nearby. The bear would then be skinned and the hide used to cover the frame, the hair being inside. Cutting up the carcass, the hunter would load the meat in the boat and, guiding himself with a pole, float down the river to the Iliuk Arm. There, or at Brooks

River, he would be met by his family or friends in a motor-driven boat, which, because of its draft, would not be usable in the swift, shallow Savonoski River.

Through most of the twentieth century, there were hardly any written reports of bears fishing for salmon at Brooks, mostly because so few people went there. By the 1960s and 1970s, there were a few bears there. Now there are many. But it would be short-sighted to say that this change alone proves that the large numbers of bears now using Brooks are an unnatural aberration, or even to say that Cahalane's account is somehow proof of native people's ability or inclination to keep local bear numbers low. The twentieth century is far too late in the region's white history to display an undisturbed setting in which native animals and people are necessarily interacting as they had three hundred or more years ago. By 1900 whites and native people had already been affecting one another's behaviors and land uses for more than a century. Populations had shifted, reasons for living in certain locations had changed, old cultural imperatives were muted or simply destroyed. Firearms and other European technologies were commonplace. Cahalane's story of the bear hunter is intriguing and revealing, but it isn't proof of anything in the bigger picture. Brooks River in 1940, or even in 1900, was no more likely to have been pristine than Brooks River in 2000.

This shortage of information on what prewhite Brooks River was like is why Birkedal's attempt to re-create the scene from the archaeological and anthropological record is so important. Through it we may get a truer glimpse of an earlier Brooks River, one that we should care about because it might be considerably different from the "wild" setting we admire so much there today.

Many state and federal lands—parks, forests, monuments, and so on—were set aside to preserve some version of wilderness values, or to protect nature in its primitive state. Recent scholars, especially in archaeology and environmental history, have pointed out that though these goals were well intentioned, they are not as easily honored as was once thought. What are we preserving here? If we hope to preserve, as National Park Service policy long expressed it, a vignette of primitive America, we are not fully succeeding because the Indians aren't out there doing their part.

It is a conversation that almost immediately bogs down in a morass of conflicting opinions, beginning with the long-standing and apparently irresolvable argument over whether humans should be considered part of nature. Very quickly we are not discussing archaeology or history; we are arguing religion. If humans are in some sense judged to be superfluous to the conservation of a setting, then Brooks without significant human food-gathering activities is still in some way "natural." But if humans must be considered an integral and essential part of a wild scene, then the evidence marshaled by Birkedal suggests that Brooks is arguably incomplete. If we wish to restore the prehistoric influences of humans on the setting at Brooks, are we not obligated to employ only the technologies available to them? If so, which technologies, from which period of the past several thousand years, should be allowed? Or is the real goal just to do something similar to what they did, in which case using rifles and monofilament gill nets would accomplish this as well as spears and weirs? If we choose to embark on such a perilous enterprise—seeking to replicate the effects of another culture at another time upon a landscape today—who gets to decide all these important questions? And why won't they do what *I* want?

Predictably, the new perspectives on prewhite North America are attractive to all sorts of advocacy groups. There is an opportunity for everyone to advance his or her own agenda: "Indians hunted in these national park lands for thousands of years, therefore I (Joe White Guy) should be allowed to hunt there today. After all, I'm just replacing the lost influences of Indians." Or, "If all you're trying to do is take some salmon out of the river like the ancient people did, can't we just count the ones that the modern sportfishermen take and call it good?" Or, in keeping with the long Alaskan tradition of objection to the very existence of the park, "The loss of these aboriginal influences makes the whole exercise of preserving this wilderness a charade, because it is no longer true to its prehistory, and therefore the park should be abolished." Many of these arguments are transparent or silly.

But other cases are enormously intriguing. In recent decades in the United States, thanks to new legislation protecting and reaffirming their ancestral and treaty rights, Native Americans have been gradually reenfranchised in the debates over land management and are now expressing strong interests in restoring some of their own effects, or in having new ones. The relationships between many tribes and nearby public lands are changing, and will continue to do so. In each instance, a unique ecological situation will demand unique answers. In Alaska, the Alaska National Interest Lands Conservation Act of 1980, which affirmed the rights of native people to continue subsistence hunting and fishing on various park lands (though not at Brooks specifically), has generated great controversy and challenged all parties, especially the native people themselves and the public land managers, to deal with a daunting array of local ecological and social questions.

I suspect that many whites, having given the idea of restoring native influences to federal wild lands a few moments' thought, are attracted to the romantic image of modern American Indians, dressed in picturesque buckskin, winging spears into herds of caribou and running bison off cliffs like their ancestors did. But at least some of the native people themselves find this annoyingly condescending. Throughout North America, their cultures have evolved in the past two centuries and now include stainless steel rifles, snowmobiles, and many other tools. They don't feel obliged to abandon all these conveniences just to satisfy some Euroamerican concept of wild lands as a kind of Indian fantasy camp. But managers of those lands are necessarily concerned with replicating in some general way the effects of precisely those earlier technologies. The uneasiness of the conversation is heightened by all the non-Indians who would regard Indian access to these lands for hunting and gathering as exclusionary and undemocratic, whatever the legislative mandate of the lands may be. (In Alaska, ANILCA gave subsistence rights not only to native people, but to many non-native rural people as well.)

I cannot even guess how this will go, but it has seemed to me that getting the Native Americans back into the mix of opinions and attitudes has been enormously helpful. Besides the justice of giving them a hearing, and the added wisdom they bring, they have heightened the attention paid to spirituality, which is often the first casualty once a case gets to court and arguments devolve into haggles over statistics and legalities. Native people bring a spiritual perspective of undeniable legitimacy to the table. They simply will not let spiritual values be ignored. Among the reasons I think this is a priceless contribution is that eventually it might improve receptivity to the spiritual values that are so important to the rest of us.

At Brooks, it seems likely to me that at least some of the time over the past few thousands years, native people did indeed affect the way bears used the river. But as interesting as that information is, it poses the same questions now being asked about many other areas. In order to honor its legal mandates to protect a wild ecosystem in Katmai National Park and Preserve, is the National Park Service also obligated to replicate the influence of the area's ancient human occupants as well? Are humans to be defined, in this respect at least, as an essential part of nature? If so, knowing that over time human influences must have varied substantially and may at times have been absent, how do managers decide what they should be now? If the National Park Service leadership chooses not to replicate those influences, are they enforcing the existence of an "unnatural" situation at Brooks River, or are they just choosing to replicate a time when human influences were absent? The cynical question might be this: Rather than being a pristine vignette of wildness, is Brooks Falls something like a huge birdfeeder, where we've selected our favorite parts of nature and cultivated a convenient way to enjoy them?

The wilderness thinker, whether purist or pragmatist, finds much to wonder about at Brooks, and for that matter, at other Alaskan bear-viewing areas. For thousands of years, native people had a fluid, evolving life here, subject to ongoing environmental variations as well as to changes brought about by new technologies, such as the arrival of the bow and arrow after millennia of spears and atlatls. More than two centuries ago, whites began to reengineer the relationship native people had with the land, thereby having a ripple effect throughout the Alaska Peninsula ecosystem. A century or so ago, whites began industrial-scale harvest of the Bristol Bay salmon runs, so that long before the sockeyes even reached the Brooks River, the size or character of the run was changed.

Early in the 1900s, the people of the United States created a national monument that eventually made it easier for bears to gather at Brooks by excluding certain native human influences on the local landscape. By the same act of creating the monument, we protected the bears throughout the park from human hunting. At the same time, hunting of bears and other animals outside the park, both by native people and by whites, continued, with unknown effects on the movements and habits of bears whose traditional ranges may have involved both park and nonpark lands. Then, most recently, we habituated the bears at Brooks so they would put up with us and let us wander around right in there with them. We did some of these things on purpose and others inadvertently, and, at least in the case of Brooks River, a lot of us are very happy with the result. But contentment with how things are going should not relieve us from occasionally asking ourselves to think more deeply about what we see here. Is this wildness? Is this wilderness? Is this the "park idealism" that Murie, quoted at the beginning of this chapter, was speaking so passionately about and that should make visitors feel "a little more worthy"?

I find these questions endlessly engaging. Whenever we struggle to peel away the layers of preference and perspective to better understand our relationship with nature, we're doing good work. Whenever we are compelled to look harder at things we have taken for granted, we will be the better for it. But I suspect that the short answer to such questions is that Murie's version of park idealism is very close to what is happening right now at Brooks. For a host of interacting reasons, including commerce, Brooks will probably continue to host as many bears as are willing to come. I will be amazed if the American public, through its courts, its legislation, and its designated managers, ever decides to change that. So far, I find that a good thing.

The environmental philosopher Holmes Rolston has suggested that wildness exists not as an absolute, but on a spectrum. Places are not either wild or tame; they are more or less wild. When I have lived in town, my lawn may not have been a wilderness, but it was more wild than my neighbor's lawn. If asked to give my best defense of Brooks as it is—no commercial or subsistence fishing, bears habituated to human presence and given priority in all fishing situations—I would couch it in those relative terms. Several rare and essential elements of a wild setting are in place. There are salmon that have just completed an epic journey whose course is the result of many thousands of years of evolution. There are brown bears, whose presence is also the result of many thousands of years of local residence and adaptation, fishing precisely as their instincts and learning enable them to. There is a robust wild environment—an extended community of other native plants and animals stretching for many miles in all directions, providing a superb backdrop for the scene. (Just the relative lack of non-native plants makes Katmai a fabulously whole wilderness compared with almost all of the lower forty-eight's landscapes.) By these objective measures, Brooks is an incredibly wild place, about as "real" as wildness gets on our planet. If, because of human absences and human actions, there is also a faint touch of theater—a hint of the managed spectacle—the twinge of regret I feel in acknowledging these flaws just keeps me honest and doesn't materially reduce the wonder. In fact, it increases the opportunity for wonder, because it gives more room to stimulate thought.

Of course, if asked, I could make just as powerful an argument *against* the current situation. I could say that my argument on behalf of the present arrangement is just the rhetoric of convenience—that if we were a brave enough society, we could do something much more vividly authentic here, something that would stretch our intellectual and emotional resources and give us correspondingly greater rewards. That would be an easy argument to make in the abstract, but a harder argument to defend when it came to the specifics of applying a braver management strategy, whatever it is.

But even if I felt that strongly about it, I would not expect it to make any difference. Considering the slow pace of progress so far, we will be doing well—in fact, heroically well—if we just straighten out the safety issues and provide better protection for the buried treasures of those former fishermen. If we need something more to worry about, we can concentrate on ensuring the long-term survival of the salmon, whose safety out in the open ocean is nowhere near as good as it is once they enter the park.

On our way north through the Yukon in late May, Henry and I stopped in Carmacks at the Northern Tutchone Interpretive Center, which is staffed by local First Nation (the Canadians' equivalent term for Native American) people. The young woman who led us around the outdoor exhibits told us a remarkable story: Her family knows of two mammoths or mastodons killed within the past five hundred years. One of these deaths occurred so recently that the animal was killed with a bullet. This was a thoughtful person, who at other points during our visit made it clear that she regarded some traditional beliefs about unknown animals to be at least potentially allegorical, but who considered the mammoth deaths to be a matter of fact.

The nearly unanimous scientific opinion, based on many archaeological and paleontological investigations and a vast amount of related theorizing, study, and debate, is that North America's mammoths were gone about eleven thousand years ago, and the last mastodons about seven thousand years ago. (A hearty and rewarding debate has been conducted for many years about the extent to which the sudden extinction of these and other late-Pleistocene species was the result of human hunting by the ancestors of the young woman who gave us the tour.) The last known nearby holdouts were an isolated population of mammoths on Wrangel Island, near the Siberian coast, which might have persisted until thirty-seven hundred years ago. The long-ago extinction of these animals is not even an issue among scientific authorities.

Ancient North American proboscidians hold a profound fascination for the public, and as a member of that group, I admit that I am charmed by the possibility that science is wrong and the young woman at Carmacks is right. And I am not the only one. There is a long tradition of hopefulness on this topic. In his *Notes on the State of Virginia* (1785), that insatiably curious naturalist Thomas Jefferson repeatedly alluded to "the traditionary testimony of the Indians, that this animal still exists in the northern and western parts of America." By the time of the Lewis and Clark expedition, 1804 to 1806, Jefferson may have had doubts about this, though he did vaguely direct the expedition to watch for remains of "rare or extinct" creatures, but under his direction, Clark spent considerable time collecting fossils of these creatures. In the late 1800s, Alaskan newspapers more or less straight-facedly reported a number of sightings and eyewitness accounts of live mammoths. Alaskan writer Ed Ferrell gathered some of these, along with similarly disreputable tales of lost gold mines, ghosts, and hidden wilderness civilizations, in *Strange Stories of Alaska and the Yukon* (1996). Sometimes the idea has even entered the mainstream of public attention. In *Jubal Sackett* (1985), one of the earliest episodes of Louis L'Amour's apparently endless series of novels about the fictitious Sackett family, the hero travels to the Rocky Mountains near the head of the Arkansas River in the 1620s. There he befriends a bison bull, and the two of them fight and kill a huge mammoth. L'Amour even provides a defiant author's note at the end of the book, defending his belief in the continued existence of these animals into recent times. Mammoths surviving into the historic period is a topic of considerable durability out there on the fringes of human belief, relegated to those same remote forests where Sasquatch also drifts in and out of the shadows.

As I say, the scientists are quite firm on this subject. They are confident that the animals died out thousands of years ago, and their case is, by their standards, quite strong. I am not qualified to challenge their findings, and I don't question many specifics of their interpretations. Nor am I aware of any of the sort of evidence that they require to contradict the prevailing view that these wonderful animals were gone a long time ago. But in *Red Earth, White Lies: Native Americans and the Myth of Scientific Fact* (1995), Vine Deloria, Jr., makes a forceful case that scientists have too narrow a view of what constitutes evidence—that substantial amounts of knowledge and wisdom about mastodons and other now-vanished creatures have survived in Indian traditions that scientists simply don't know how to use or respect.

And my sympathies lie with the people who question the scientific view. I will not surrender my hard-earned sense of empiricism. I will still require some kind of concrete proof—a freshly excavated mastodon skull with an obvious bullet hole in the forehead would be nice—but for some reason, I'm willing to give the supporters of the mastodons-just-died-out-recently opinion more room than I normally give such long shots. I have little trouble rejecting the old newspapers and magazines and Louis L'Amour, but the calm conviction of that young woman demands my respect. Perhaps it's merely a matter of culture, and I'm just more willing to distrust white people because I know them better.

These kinds of conflicts among the views of different cultures came to mind often at Brooks, and not just because I was so aware of the archaeological complications there. I thought of them while fishing. Like the scientific biography of the mammoth, the modern regulation of sportfishing reveals striking differences between native people and their more recently arrived companions on the North American landscape.

The copy of the Yukon "Sport Fishing Regulations Summary" I was given when I bought my license in Watson Lake has a section entitled "Recreational Fishing, a First Nation View." The section introduces a controversy over sportfishing, and then quotes several First Nation people on the matter, as follows:

> You may be surprised to learn that many Yukon Indian people don't feel good about live-release fishing. This practice is helping us conserve fish stocks and build a sustainable fishery, right? So what's the problem?
>
> The problem, from a First Nation perspective, is respect for the fish. In practice, this means you take the fish you need for food and then stop fishing. It

means you don't play with fish and then let them go. Here's what some Yukon Indian people have said about recreational fishing and live-release fishing:

"It (recreational fishing) is a spiritual quest. People are trying to fulfill their spiritual needs, and that's good. The value is in getting out there in nature's creation. It's not in the fish."
—Mark Wedge, Carcross-Tagish First Nation

"I watch these fishermen on TV. They catch a big lake trout and lift him up out of the water. Then they measure him and take a picture and horse around with him. They take the hook out and let him go. Then they catch him again. How do you think that fish feels?"
—Jessie Scarff, Kwanlin Dun First Nation

"It's hard to put into words. Underlying (our view) is respect. Respect for animals. Respect for fish."
—David Dickson, Liard First Nation

"The fish comes to you as a gift. It's offering its life to you. And if you don't accept it, that's an insult. Sooner or later the fish will stop coming to you."
—Mark Wedge, Carcross-Tagish First Nation

"The foundation of our thinking is respect. And that's what we carry to you. Respect. For humans, animals, trees and all life. . . . (The earth) belongs to all of us, and we are all part of it. And we have to make sure it's still here for our children."
—Millie Pauls, Ross River Dene Council

Since its appearance as a management approach more than fifty years ago, "live-release" fishing, which is called "catch-and-release" in the United States, has been heralded as the salvation of countless fisheries. To some extent, it just reinforced long-standing practices among many sportsmen, who threw the small ones back to catch again when they get bigger, but it reached further than that and eventually amounted, like disapproval of snagging, to a significant alteration in the culture of the sport. As fishery resources were threatened with overuse and collapse of fish populations, it became obvious that saving some part of the experience might be the best hope left.

For many years—and this is still so in many places—the answer to overfishing was to dump huge numbers of hatchery-raised fish into public waters. At that stage, fishermen and managers still insisted that the killing of fish was essential for the experience to be complete. But as we learned more about fisheries, especially trout waters, it became clear that such practices were often harmful to whatever native fish populations might have been in place when the hatchery fish were released into the water. As "wild," stream-bred fish came to have a higher value among sportsmen, "put-and-take" fishing came to be seen as a cheap thrill, rather like a bird-watcher going to a zoo and adding all the rare African and Asian birds he sees in the cages to his life list. A fish whose forebears have been living in the water for many generations and could therefore be assumed to know its way around was recognized as a superior challenge to the angler. And as respect for the wholeness of native ecosystems has increased, a higher aesthetic premium has been placed on catching native fish that evolved in the setting. This respect for the native setting and its inhabitants is still a minority view in many parts of North

America, but it has made an enormous difference in the direction of modern fisheries management.

Wild, native, nonstocked fish can only stand so much harvest. Catch-and-release fishing, though it no longer could feed people fish, did at least assure them of a chance to catch some. Because it was so obviously successful as a conservation strategy—frequently touted because it also kept all those fish in the water, where they could play their roles in the food chain both as predators and as prey—it has grown in popularity and public appeal. Yellowstone Park, which helped popularize the concept in the 1970s, is now in good part a catch-and-release fishery, especially for native fish species. A skilled angler can park his car within a hundred feet of the Yellowstone River, walk over to it, and catch and release fifty or more trout of fourteen to eighteen inches in a few hours, a phenomenally rare experience on today's hard-fished public waters. People come to Yellowstone from all over the world, and they take the lesson home.

But the most important lesson may be about the nature of the sport of fishing. Catch-and-release regulations showed that fishing did not have to involve killing. Fishermen had a choice that hunters did not. As my friend Bud Lilly, one of the West's best-known outfitters and guides, has put it, "It's a lot like golf—you don't have to eat the ball to have a good time."

But for much of its existence, catch-and-release has also had its critics. I first encountered one in Yellowstone about twenty-five years ago, when a German visitor indignantly objected to my releasing fish. I did not realize at the time that Europeans were proceeding faster than we were in their protection of what were seen as the rights of the fish, and I was shocked that someone could object to a practice that made such good sense in so many ways. At that time, I was new to the sport of fly-fishing, I didn't think trout tasted all that good anyway, and I was just thrilled that I could fish without interfering with the food habits of the local eagles, osprey, otters, bears, and other fishers out there. I thought I was on the moral high road, and this man insisted that I was in the gutter.

There is plenty of easy criticism of the practice of catch-and-release. "So let me get this straight. What you do is, you hook these animals in the mouth and drag them from their environment, right? For all you know they're feeling terrible pain; sometimes you hook them in the tongue, for heaven's sake. Their frantic struggles, which you seem to find so satisfying and fulfilling, are all the proof any rational person should need that the fish are terrified. Okay, maybe they can't experience terror with the same level of intellectual and emotional sophistication that we can, but they're doing an excellent imitation of a creature scared entirely out of its mind—why else would they willingly jump again and again from the water into a world where they can't even breathe? So then, after you've put them through that, you don't even *eat* them? It's all just a joke? You just do it for *fun?* You torture these fish and call that sport? How can you *do* that?"

Sport, like the church or the stock exchange, is an easy institution to lampoon. In the case of the blood sports, the quickest path to that caricature is to equate it with fun. Sport is an ancient thing, like music or cooking or art. Those anonymous artists who created such powerful portraits of animals in the caves of France thousands of years ago probably also engaged in sport. No doubt they had something that could be called fun when they were painting, or even when they were hunting—and certainly when they were eating. But to say they simply had fun does not do justice to the thing they did, or how it must have felt, or what it may have meant to them. The exhilaration of a personal gift that has been painstakingly built into a skill and then exercised with surpassing mastery is far more than fun. Or perhaps it is just the highest form of fun. There was no break or distinction between the artist painting the animal in the cave, and the artist then participating in the hunt of that animal, and the artist then participating in the killing and eating of that animal. These things were all parts of one act. Perhaps none of us today can achieve that wholeness—that integration of so many mysteries—but through study and my own art and my own contacts with the animal, I am willing to piece together whatever of it I can.

Others no longer are. In an essay called "Catch and Deny" in his provocative, eloquent book *Heart of Home* (1997), Ted Kerasote interviewed a variety of intelligent sportsmen on the matter of catch-and-release, some of whom have finally quit fishing entirely, either because the scientific evidence that fish do feel pain is piling uncomfortably on their shoulders, or because of some vague fellow feeling with the fish, or just because it seemed like time. Ted, who has said that "the wading, the casting, the stalking, the picking, the plowing, are the ceremonial means to procure nature's Eucharist," concluded with the uneasiness shared by most of his interviewees, and by me.

We do everything we can to reduce the potential for permanently harming the fish. We debarb our hooks in the hope that this will ease the release of the fish, though many scientific studies tell us it will make no difference in the very small mortality of released fish (three or four out of a hundred will die from the experience). We approach a limited sort of mysticism when we experiment with flies whose hooks are bent closed; unable to hook the fish at all, we want to see if just the strike of the fish is enough of a contact (sometimes, almost . . .). We spend more and more time watching, and less and less time casting. We suspect, somewhat darkly, that we know where this might be headed: to a day when society reverts for a time back to catch-only-if-you-mean-to-kill—a time that will ironically echo the earlier excesses of anglers who killed all too much—and then on to a time when sportfishing goes the way of hunting, as an archaic thing people are embarrassed to admit their grandparents did. But we persist because we know, we know damned well, that we are on to something important and that in some troublesome, aching way this catching of fish matters beyond all doubt and all reason.

I recently attended a small conference on the importance of protecting wild places, a sort of roundtable discussion in which about twenty devoted conservationists were comparing notes on things that they found especially powerful in their own experiences of nature. After several others had spoken, including a hunter or two, I mentioned something about the connection to be had with the natural world through fishing. I used the example of that taking effect—when I first felt the strike and pull of a fish—as one of those powerful moments in our contact with nature. I think this was okay with them, but in the context of my comments, I mentioned releasing the fish. Instantly some of the other conferees were on the attack. One referred to what I was doing as "catch-and-maim." They were quite upset about this and kept asking, "How can you *do* that?" Their self-righteousness so overwhelmed my own that I not only shut up, but I left the conference soon after, just quietly slipping away during the next break. They were well-meaning, and they were doing good work, but I didn't belong there. I had been caught so off guard that I simply had no idea what else I might say that would provoke another ambush like that. I had mistakenly assumed we were on the same side.

It wasn't that I hadn't heard it all before. I'm sure I could have stated their arguments as well as they did, having studied the evolution of attitudes toward wildlife more than any of them had, and having also had abundant time, while catching and releasing thousands of fish—looking again and again into those myopic, unblinking, baffled eyes—to reflect on the moral and emotional implications of what I was doing. I knew what they were talking about. What was so hard to take was the absolute intractability of their attack.

"How can you do that?" is not really a question. In order to be a question, a sentence must give some evidence that the speaker is interested in the answer. It is, rather like the questions Henry and I were asked by that first Alaskan we met, only a device. I am not sure I've ever had a genuine conversation with someone who was outraged about catch-and-release, or about the hard realities and violence involved in sportfishing generally. Ideas are not to be exchanged under such circumstances, only rhetorical blows. The question "How can you do that?" is really a statement: "I could not do that, therefore you are a brutish fool."

Even if someone asked it hoping for an answer, it isn't an honest, fair question. It is as if, when the woman in Carmacks told me about her family's knowledge of recently killed mammoths, I had asked, "How can you *believe* that?" It is a simplistic challenge to a complex and probably unexplainable view of the world. I could ask my questioners the same question about a hundred things that are dear to them—"You drive a car? You pick living wildflowers? You're a Cubs fan? How can you *do* that?"—and they would object that these questions are too big

187

for a quick answer; that their behavior in these activities is the product of their culture, and when they do these things they are responding to complex impulses that I am cheapening by such a superficial question. And yet they seem to find in my inability to instantly and completely answer their question about catch-and-release to be proof of my wrongness and—more important to them, I think—their superior sensitivity.

But there is more to the failure of their question. When they ask, "How can you do that?" and I try to imagine my life without all those hundreds of glowing days along wild mountain streams all over North America—all the beauty I've absorbed, all the shared and remembered wonder, all the gratitude I've felt not just to the fish, but to the rivers they glorify with their presence—I can only turn the question back to them. In my view of the world, and my view of the fish, I am tempted to answer their question by asking them, "Oh, but how can you *not* do that?"

But that's not fair, either. It's nearly as bigoted as their original question. If I had to try to answer their question in a meaningful way, rather than in the same quarrelsome and pointless mood in which they asked it, I might say things like this: These are matters of the spirit. You may call it a cop-out or a dodge if you like, but these are mysteries in the highest sense of the word. Because they are so insubstantial at the same time that they are so important, I rarely ease off in my testing and questioning of them. I pay attention really hard. I ask myself the same question and I expect an answer. Having told you that, I will tell you that I don't suppose I ever entirely release a fish. I may not eat it, but that does not mean I take nothing from it before I let it go. What I take may be impossible to describe to you, because each time it is different, and because you apparently aren't prepared to deal with the possibility that nature affects each of us uniquely and therefore might accommodate different ways of connecting with it. What happens is between me and the fish, between me and what my conscience requires of me. I am not responsible to your conscience; my own makes me work hard enough. Ultimately, I suspect that "how I can do that" is none of your business, and it is only because I have better manners than you do that I am willing to stand here and let you heap your unreasoning abuse on me.

These criticisms of sportfishing came to mind when I read those quotations in the Yukon fishing regulations. Those of us who are at all sensitized to American society's clumsy yet delicate relationship with native people know the hesitation with which one disagrees with any tribal belief or tradition. First Nation people and Native Americans may not have a corner on the market in respecting the earth, but they have an undeniable and painfully earned voice that one is hesitant to contradict. When our behavior is criticized by these people, the criticism is often couched in terms that make it clear that the hurt is more theirs than ours. At the first hint of criticism from people with their extended tradition of wisdom about such things, we tend to go up on our tiptoes and wish only to ease away from further offense.

Still, when a First Nation person objects to catch-and-release fishing and asks, "How do you think that fish feels?" it does sound as if he is asking his version of "How can you do that?" But because of who he is and what he represents, I am inclined to try as hard as I can to give him a respectful answer. I sense the same potent brew of religion and emotion in his question that I sensed from the white conservationists who challenged me on this same point, but I also sense my own heightened desire not to offend this questioner.

Even so, I am not sure I can give him any more helpful an answer than I gave the whites. The glib answer, the one I resist but that I think he will hear from many sportsmen if he asks them how the fish feels about being repeatedly caught and released, runs something like this: "Well, if I were a fish, and if I were able to think at all, I would much prefer being released to being killed."

And the glib response to *that* answer might be, "But you're not a fish, and you have no idea what a fish might think, much less prefer."

The question itself can thus become a barrier between the cultures. In the modern science of animal consciousness, much of the debate seems to involve whether or not we can even find a way to comprehend how another species' mind works, much less identify what kinds of things might interest that mind. While native people may feel a certain confidence in their understanding of what another species thinks or feels, non-native people (at least those who are scientifically educated) are more likely to bog down in ruminations over our frustrating inability to know that species' mind at all.

But this is not a scientific dialogue, is it? The native person who is offended by the sight of someone releasing a fish is stating a religious conviction and a moral certainty. The white sportsman is then pursuing the issue by his own logical and ethical lights. (I'd love to see some analyses of how catch-and-release would fit in Christian doctrine.) Meanwhile, the animal behaviorist is disassembling the issue to try to establish finer and finer facts about the fish itself. And when they've all finished speaking, the native person's faith, the white man's logic, and the scientist's conclusions are all still standing and all still somewhat defiant of each other.

There is much more going on in these disagreements than merely a clash between people who have a deeply felt value system about wild animals and people who don't. There are conflicting value systems in action here. But, as I have perhaps revealed through my heightened need not to offend the native questioner, the modern sensibility has led us to respect some value systems more than others.

For example, implicit in such conflicts today is the idea that native people, because they have been holding to their beliefs and practices since ancient times, and because they are often so much more closely connected to nature in their everyday lives, deserve special respect or consideration. I favor this argument regularly.

But I am not unaffected by some counterarguments. One counterargument might ask, "So what if my attitudes and behavior aren't based on such long traditions? Why does that necessarily make them less worthy of respect?" In other words, why does long-standing practice (and, of course, the long-standing religious traditions behind that practice) make a person's approach to wildlife "better?" Where does the superior authority we grant the native person originate? I have my own ideas about this, and they have to do with my suspicion that a society's wisdom is cumulative, and that traditions and beliefs that grew over a long period of time from intimate association with nature are likely worthy of great respect and attention. But nobody else is necessarily required to see it that way, or to think less of their own values because they are products of some other process.

As it happens, there are very few perspectives on the harvest of wildlife that are less than ancient. Certainly my view is the result of many centuries of several white cultures' applying their own beliefs to the use of natural resources. If I can trace my personal preference for how to treat these animals back a thousand years or so in Europe, does that help my case? Perhaps it does, but I'm not sure why it should. (It is odd that I sometimes seem more eager to honor the native person's traditions than to honor my own, but I suppose this is partly because I know that my European ancestors did a lot of stupid and embarrassing things that I would never dream of honoring.) Would somehow relating my fishing more closely to my religious beliefs or moral code help? It might, but again, who gets to address the irresolvable question of which belief or code is superior, and which is inferior?

Not the people who wrote the Yukon fishing regulations I quoted earlier. They diplomatically and I think wisely bypassed the moral issue, instead emphasizing that "live-release" fishing should not be seen as only the freeing of a fish—that it should instead be seen as the postponement of the killing of that fish until it has grown to a more useful size and can be caught again. This keeps the dialogue on a practical level. In the end, the fish still gets to die.

I wonder if there is a way to honor these opposing traditions, perhaps even to honor their differences. I wonder that because I think we have more in common than we are admitting. Earlier, I mentioned the extent to which we now know that native people in North America influenced their environments. For some years there has been a vigorous academic dialogue over the idea of the "ecological Indian." This concept, which has great popularity in white society, portrays native people as natural (almost instinctive) conservationists whose understanding of ecological principals placed them in perfect harmony with their surroundings—a balance that was not upset until whites arrived in North America. But since the 1960s, scholars, resource managers, native people, and advocates of many management approaches have reconsidered the relationship of native people to their environment. Anthropologist Shepard Krech III, in *The Ecological Indian* (1999), confronts the remarkably complex issues surrounding the question of whether or not native North American people were in fact the "original ecologists," or "environmentalists," or even "conservationists." These matters have generated a heated and many-sided debate. Native people do not agree among themselves, any more than do non-native people.

But even after hearing these debates and disagreements, and even after discovering how often native people are at odds with *white* environmentalists, one is left with no doubt that native culture and religion are profoundly entwined with the workings of the natural world. When it comes to nature-based spirituality, the prevailing public view seems to be that most white people are lightweights by comparison.

In my wide and unstructured exploration of American history, I have encountered many early accounts of native people harvesting this or that animal, often in great numbers. The literature is full of descriptions of buffalo jumps, deer and elk drives, and fish kills that would meet most modern definitions of "industrial scale." Most of these descriptions inspire my admiration: these people were extremely skilled gatherers and users of wild animal protein, and what they were doing was often mortally dangerous. In several western states and provinces, I have visited buffalo-jump sites, where large numbers of animals were driven over cliffs and killed—a sudden and no doubt wonderful bounty for the people who conducted the hunt. Anyone with even a modest familiarity with American history knows about these harvests, and understands the necessity for them. But, except for our continued slaughter of wild marine creatures, we in modern

American society freed ourselves from this necessity long ago, when we domesticated animals that we could kill more easily and in even greater numbers. We, at least the hunters among us, do still kill wild animals, but usually just one or two a year (deer, for example) or in strictly regulated small numbers (sport fish and game birds).

But larger kills are still an important part of life for some North Americans, especially native people. In *Last Light Breaking* (1993), Nick Jans's memoir of life among Alaskan Inupiat Eskimos, there is a description of an Eskimo family netting fish in a tributary of the Kobuk. Jans is helping manage the net, or trying to:

> I run two hitches around a drift log and sprint the fifty yards to Minnie, who has her end nearly in. "Look, we have fish!" she says. The curve of water before us is boiling with them—hundreds, no, thousands. I can feel them surging against the net, a heavy, vibrant pulse that jerks at my shoulders. At my feet, fish are throwing themselves ashore, flopping against my boots, and falling back into the maelstrom.

I read this description with the ears, attitudes, and heart of a white guy whose ancestors spent the last millennium efficiently manipulating the aquatic environments of Europe before coming to North America. They participated in precisely this kind of harvest, using the same methods and even more comprehensive ones. In the same millennium, they developed the sporting practices and codes to which I still adhere. Often the same people participated in both the utilitarian harvest and the sport; and over time, they may have become indistinguishable. I therefore must keep in mind that whatever I choose to do out there on the river, I am a product of intellectually forceful traditions about how to deal with wild animals, and I will make my choices largely out of those traditions.

Indeed, as I described earlier, I actively participate in the continuing evolution of those traditions. In a few cases, I have consciously rejected the preferred behaviors of earlier generations because they no longer seemed to suit the needs of the modern world. This change I've made reaches far beyond the specifics of sporting practice. Certainly, for example, most of my ancestors did not share my passion for wildness in nature.

There is nothing novel about this process that I have participated in. It is one small part of how culture changes. But the changes do not mean that I have no culture or that I am divorced from tradition. Rather, I am the latest manifestation of a singularly dynamic tradition. Starting with inherited attitudes, then adding an intensive if informal exposure to ecological sciences and an equally intensive introduction to the aesthetics of nature appreciation, I have arrived at a way of seeing these fish and their world that is both deeply felt and spiritually vital.

I firmly disagree with those who think that activities like sport are mere matters of lifestyle rather than serious elements of culture. I think on, and wonder over, and read about, and fight for the protection of wildness all year. A day does not pass without me thinking about wild fish and other wild things, usually gratefully and always with admiration. Call it what you will—daydreaming, reflection, worship—it is a central part of my life. I would not dream of claiming that it connects me as fully or correctly with nature as any other person, native or non-native. I wouldn't know how to measure such a connection, and I'm not sure why I should try. I'm not convinced that a competition for spiritual championship—who is the holiest?—is going to help us here.

From this personal angle on the world, when I first read Jans's story of netting fish, I experienced an unexpected shock. It was not the shock that these people killed so many fish, because I knew they needed them to eat or sell and because they've been doing it for thousands of years. To me, at least, their fishing has a feeling of great rightness about it, and I celebrate that there are still places where fish are abundant enough, and people scarce enough, that such harvests can still go on. No, I wasn't shocked because they killed so many. I was shocked because the process sounded well, just a little disrespectful.

When I read Jans's description, I thought this: What a luxurious glut of beautiful individual creatures! I have waited half my life to reach a place where I could cast into such an abundance of life, and my deepest hope is that I might catch a few, one at a time, to savor their power and wildness as single, unique animals. I would never need so many, and I would never want to harm them so much.

The key to this shock of mine is that in one way, I was right. If it had been me killing that many fish, it would have been disrespectful. Kill a thousand fish at once? How could I *do* that? But it wasn't me. It was people for whom I regard such a kill as appropriate. They aren't responsible to my conscience.

To many native people, as one of the First Nation people quoted above so perfectly put it, the gift of the fish is its life. But to me, the gift of the fish is to allow me to feel for a few moments the surge and energy of that life. They kill it out of respect. I let it go out of respect.

Therefore I am not sure that the ancient buffalo hunter, or the First Nation man, or the Inupiat woman, and I are quite as different as we might at first appear. When I hooked a salmon at Brooks, I also felt the "heavy vibrant pulse that jerks at my shoulders," and I imagine that the pulse is probably about the same one and has the same effect on the heart and soul of the fisherman, whatever finally happens to the fish that causes it.

Someone other than me can try to decide which of our approaches is the more morally defensible or more fully honors nature. I'm sure I don't know. Someone other than me is welcome to pass judgment on the world's millions of inarticulate "sportsmen," from the beeriest fish-hogs to the most talented high-tech televised fishing celebrities, but I don't pretend to know what's going on in their heads, or to be able to tell which ones are secretly living their rivers too.

But neither do I take kindly to the presumption that I don't respect these fish just because I happen to show my respect differently than some other people do. The hardest part of respectful fishing is not in respecting the fish; it is in respecting each other as fishermen.

These same issues of respect come up at Brooks. For decades, the philosophically minded have been wondering about fishing in national parks. Twenty years ago I wrote an article in *Rod & Reel* magazine in which I was apparently the first person to expose most anglers to this question: In a national park, where all animals are supposed to receive equal protection, why do we allow some to be subjected to the violent attention of visitors while others are protected from any such treatment? There are plenty of people capable of enjoying fish the same way they enjoy other wild animals, which is to say the way we enjoy the bears at Brooks—just by watching them. Fish-watching is not that difficult, and it opens a window on a world of wonders we have too long denied ourselves. National parks, because their legislative mandates amount to "equal-rights amendments" for all living creatures, are ripe for legal actions by people who disapprove of sportfishing, for whatever set of moral or other reasons.

Dave Bohn, whom I have already quoted on the sins of photographers, has an even longer list of sins of anglers at Katmai, and holds catch-and-release fishermen in special contempt: "I have a dark suspicion that this psychology, if written out on paper, would not make for pleasant reading." But he is also troubled, as I am sure others are, by the industrial scale of angling tourism. Speaking of the fishermen that I share the river with, he says, "There is something inherently pitiful about coming from many hundreds of miles away, catching a 'legal' limit in one of the most magnificent of the remaining wild areas on the planet, and then taking the fish home on a Boeing 707."

I wonder about this too. In the 1970s, when I first went to Vermont to serve as director of The American Museum of Fly Fishing, I met many fishermen who could afford to travel anywhere on earth and regularly did. One day, as I stood at the sink in my cottage, I thought, "Here I am rinsing out a plastic bag so I can reuse it, and these people are exploding thousands of gallons of jet fuel just to go fishing. Some explode more jet fuel to ship their dead fish home. What a curious world." Now, standing there in the Brooks River, I marveled at how eagerly I had finally become one of those fishermen, except that I had no intention of mailing a fish carcass anywhere. It's the difference between being twenty-five and being fifty, I suppose.

In our global food market, it would take some formidable accounting skills to establish the relative costs of shipping a fish home to eat and buying it "fresh" at the local grocery store. Someone, whether you or a commercial enterprise, had to explode jet fuel to ship both fish from somewhere far away. I gather that Alaskan anglers ship great numbers of fish home (nowhere else I've been are cheap Styrofoam shipping coolers so readily available). I'm not sure the dollar cost—including all "real" costs, in terms of fossil fuel production to get me to Alaska and back and to run the fishing boat as well as the jets, and so on—for shipping a few big salmon or a single halibut the size of a motor scooter home is going to be much more than buying the equivalent amount of fish meat at the store. And the intangibles—those other factors that economists struggle with so mightily, or just ignore—are complex: "This is not just some dead fish from Alaska, this is the very fish I caught that day off Homer, when we saw the whales—see, there's the picture I took on the wall and the eagle almost landed on the boat, and I dropped the rental car keys in the water, and do you remember when . . ." Dave Bohn has a point, but I'm not sure it's as confident a point as he thinks.

On the other hand, it's nice to know that while I'm busy worrying about keeping my body in one piece here at Brooks, there are so many people worrying about the well-being of my soul.

It being my fiftieth birthday, Marsha bought me a self-indulgently large dinner at the lodge. After one more enforced bear delay at the bridge, we went back to the cabin to start packing for our morning flight. We had the place to ourselves; our hosts were both away on their weekends, and a friend of theirs who had showed up unexpectedly and occupied the couch for a few days had also just left on a long backcountry hike. Nestled in, listening to the occasional rain squall rustle across the roof shingles, we relished the coziness of another twilit Katmai night. But we were both more or less ready to leave, now just waiting for the next new Alaskan thing to begin.

It was more of a success for me than for Marsha. Several days of unrelieved worrying and watchfulness about bears was a strain, as was having me wander out of sight now and then to go fishing. Her art was hard, too, because it was impossible to find a nice shady tree and sit down to draw and paint for an hour or two, when at any time your ear might be nuzzled by a brown bear. And, being a shy artist, she found that there were just too many people on the platforms for her to work comfortably and privately there. I suppose that when I went fishing and she went with me, the same problem prevailed. Normally she could concentrate on art, but at Brooks, we both were probably subconsciously assigning her some responsibility to watch my back. Despite these drawbacks, however, one of her little sketches at the falls captured that odd, engaging quality of the ears of the local bears better than any of my photographs did.

It was far from a matter of her wishing she hadn't come. We agreed that it had been an unforgettable week, one of those shared memories that somehow cement us together even more firmly. As well, it was professionally priceless for both of us, a good acquaintance with a remarkable park management situation we were much better off for having seen. But for a first visit, we had had enough, and I was already well into worrying about how the flight to Anchorage would go when we finally went to sleep.

Pilgrims

Then my heart turns to Alaska,
and freedom on the run;
I can hear her spirit calling me.

—John Denver, 1971

All morning it rained, or got ready to rain, or stopped
raining for a minute. We were supposed to fly out to
King Salmon midmorning, but a heavy fog settled in the
treetops, and nothing was moving in or out of Brooks. We
decided to go over to the lodge to wait for the plane, so with
the help of our new friends, we loaded everything on a
Cushman and headed to the river, but the sow and cub were
lounging in the middle of the bridge. We pulled the Cushman over to the back ramp of the platform and waited,
sometimes in the more comfortable Suburban parked there,
and sometimes up on the platform where we could have a
last look at the river.

The bears displayed an almost human Sunday-morning
lethargy, as though they were reading the paper and waiting
for the coffee to be done. The sow assumed her chin-resting
pose at the rail, and the cub stretched out to wait until his
mother decided to move or fish or do something else he

could whine about. Part of the current management dissatisfaction about the Brooks Camp development is that visitors can get caught like this on the wrong side of the bridge when they need to catch a plane. By moving all facilities to the south side of the river and surrendering the north side back to nature, this problem would be relieved. The bridge would be gone.

After an hour or so, Diver waded into view from upstream, coming down from the falls on his morning constitutional. The sow saw or otherwise sensed him coming and hurried her cub from the bridge, past the platform, and out toward the lakeshore. Both bears were still close, but our park service friends judged the opening sufficient, and rushed us and all our gear across the wet bridge and over to the lodge before either bear could move in.

The next time the rain stopped, I went out for a look at the lake. The surface near shore was glassy and gray, broken here and there by the quick swirls of salmon dorsals. A new wave of fish was working its way along the shore toward the mouth of the river (two days later the Anchorage paper reported that though the run was still a disaster, it was picking up its pace a little). Even after a week of fishing, I reflexively made a few mental casts. Down the beach just past the mouth of the river, the sow was crapped out on her back lazing away the morning, the cub lolling around on her big chest in hopes of a snack.

They were still there a little later, when the big float plane rounded the point under the low ceiling and eased in toward shore. We boarded quickly, and as the plane taxied out to deeper water, we could see another sow with three tiny cubs about half a mile up the beach to the north. One of us said that she must be having a busy summer.

More than once Bob Barbee suggested, in an earnest tone that I knew meant this was important, that I "really ought to go to the Alaska Fur Exchange." A few days before Marsha and I left Anchorage, we finally stopped there, on Old Seward Highway, for what proved to be as provocative and memorable an experience as any museum or library. It is a famous business, advertised as "the state's largest selection of genuine native & Alaskan-made arts & crafts," and it certainly had those in great abundance, but what engaged our attention most were the furs.

In my family, trapping was just something that was done. One of my uncles in Ohio was especially active, trapping mostly muskrats to sell the skins. I remember sneaking to his freezer out in the garage for an unauthorized fudgsicle and having to root around among all the milk cartons packed with skinned muskrat carcasses that he saved to feed his cats. I can also remember how indignant he would get when animal-rights activists, who loathe trapping, were mentioned. ("What those people don't seem to realize is that these wild animals *eat* each other. Sometimes they kill each other first, and sometimes they don't!") I have never trapped, and it sounds like nasty, unpleasant work to me, but I have never entirely given up on the idea of it, either. When I started reading what Alaskan trappers said, I recognized a kindred ambivalence. Here is the poet and essayist John Haines on the long, slow process by which one gets what one gets from the experience:

In all that harshness and cruelty there is a knowledge to be gained, a necessary knowledge, acquired in the only way it can be, from close familiarity with the creatures hunted. A knowledge of blood, of sinew and gut; of the structure and joint of muscle, the shape of the skull, the angularity, the sharpness or roundness of nose and ears and lips and teeth. There is passion in the hand that pulls the pelt and strokes the fur, confident that it knows as second nature all the hinges and recesses of the animal body. But however close that familiarity, something is always withheld; the life of the animal remains other and beyond, never completely yielding all that it is.

So much can be said about it from one conviction or another, the attitudes easily become partisan and intractible. There is the coarseness too often found in those who follow the trade, especially where mere cash is the end in mind. And yet to some fortunate individuals there have been few things more deeply attractive than this seasonal pursuit of the wild. It is life at its fullest, uncertain and demanding, but rich with expectation.

I am struck by his application of the word "intractible" here, recalling that I used the same term to describe the people who had attacked me as a fisherman. There are many people out there for whom the world holds little ambivalence; so many things are blissfully right or atrociously wrong. At times I almost envy that kind of confidence, but I seldom trust it. There are, I am certain, absolutely wrong things that happen between humans—racism, violence, any kind of cruelty—that a decent value system must abhor. But this business of applying those same values to relationships with other species, though I suspect that at heart it is one of the most noble enterprises available to us, is more troubled and problematic. Nowhere in Alaska could I feel the urgent pullings of so many partisan convictions more strongly than in the fur exchange.

Mixed in among the decorated moose antlers, engraved mammoth and walrus tusks, and smaller figurines beyond the avarice of the most ambitious home iconographer were what seemed like acres of fur. As a passionate watcher and student of wildlife, it was a kind of heaven. My craving to get a good look at a wild wolverine was almost satisfied by holding an entire bundle of their perfectly prepared pelts—so this is how that coloration works, and the neck isn't what I thought, and look how the fur lies on the leg. . . . Entire racks of foxes, sorted and bundled by color, hanging long and soft and slack and inviting; full mounts of wolves and lynx, sitting, standing, ready to walk away; wolf rugs, mouths open in the inevitable and apparently still marketable near-snarl; stacks of furs, walls of furs, toys of fur, hats of fur. Everything beckoned, required an admiring stroke.

There is ample room for ambivalence here, too. Every heaven has its hell. No doubt the whole show would horrify some. Marsha and I alternated admiration for the beauty with regret for all the death. I much prefer all these things alive, and, for all the extravagant glories of each item, I had no interest in owning any of it. Unlike Haines, I hadn't earned their possession.

The biggest question on my mind was who, especially among the tourists, would buy them. I had no trouble comfortably imagining natives and other bush Alaskans coming in to the store and buying furs to wear or otherwise use. But I was puzzled, even uneasy, about the rest of us. I admit, this might reveal some social—or at least antitourist—bias on my part that would be hard to defend, but there it was. I was curious about it. Who would wear the hats, each sporting the face of one of half a dozen species? Who will want the face of a lynx over his forehead? Who would drape this blue fox over a sofa? Who would cut this bundle of whites into trim and collars? It wasn't that I couldn't imagine such people, or that I wholly disapproved of them; after all, I don't need to know the life history of each individual animal whose meat I buy in the store, or whose hide made the belt I wear. I just wondered who they were and why they wanted these things. How far would they be from the animal and from the person who had actually gone out there somewhere in the wild country and killed it—the person whose passionate hand had peeled it off the body and attended to its preparation? How would the buyer connect to all that wildness and passion? I know the furs represent the livelihood of many people, and the price of that livelihood is a reality for countless wildlife populations. But standing there amidst all this loveliness and misery, it seemed to me that something paid for so dearly by the animal and by the person who killed it is in some way unearned by someone who contributes only "mere cash" to the deal.

It was the skins and mounts that were going to be bought as they were that most puzzled me. I suppose they are carted off to homes in Cleveland and Frankfurt and Tokyo, where they will perhaps find a place of honor or will just as likely end up in the attic, kept out of sight like the stolen trophies they seemed to be.

I didn't share the need for the furs, but I recognized the power of that need in others. The impulse behind all of this commerce in animal parts is just a variation on the urge we feel to catch—and eat, or not eat—a wild fish, or the desire we have to shoot or watch or photograph a bird, a buck, or a bear. When we see something wild, we are overcome by a powerful, even elemental covetousness, a kind of loving greed, and like every tribe and nation before us, we succumb to this yearning. We see the beauty and the freedom, and we have to reach toward it, hold it, take it home. Some of us take our effect with rifles and traps, some with rods and hooks, some with cameras and binoculars, some with watercolors, free verse, and sculpture. Some of us use the techniques and instruments of science, and, as biologist Bernd Heinrich puts it, "mount the trophy between the pages of a prominent journal." A wise and gifted few of us can take all the effect we need without leaving the house, and with nothing in our hands at all. Most of us like to think we're different from the rest, but that is largely a conceit.

This demand we place on nature is readily demeaned as the need of our species—or at least our Western culture—to control and dominate. True, we are a grasping, self-centered crowd. But that does not fully explain what is going on, even among the most crude and least feeling of us. Though the urge we feel is often expressed in proprietary ways, under that possessiveness is a need to embrace something less tangible. Tom Watkins was right: There are many kinds of trophies, and what is a trophy, after all, but the embodiment of memory? Trophies, whether hide or horn or photograph or field note or watercolor, express hope—that we have connected, that we have done something meaningful in the right way, and perhaps even that we have brought some of the wild thing's power to our hearts. Our spirits brush against others. We are touching mysteries here, and even the most crass of us cannot be unmoved. Those most proud of their sophisticated sentiments and aesthetic restraint had best be cautious about judging the rest.

In a differently valued world, this might be simpler. In a fantasy culture where everyone thought more similarly, none of us would be accusing others of cruelty, or missing the point, or bad manners, or that greatest and most damning of all modern shortcomings, insensitivity. Brooks River would still be a great thrill, but we would all realize that it doesn't take huge, rare animals to awaken our wonder, and that if our eyes and hearts are open, all nature is equal as spectacle. We would find, with Whitman, "a leaf of grass no less than the journeywork of the stars," and we would be content.

It is pleasant to think that we might be headed in that direction, and even though humanity does not seem capable of such contentment, we could give ourselves much less worthy ideals to hold up as we go.

In the meantime, Brooks River and its wild congregation suggest to me that what we really seek is authenticity. The argument over how to manage such a place does in fact take us somewhere besides the judicial system. It takes us on a journey toward understanding, even toward something like

truth. The more we talk and study and probe, the more we are able to peel away layers of misperception and artificiality and find something reliably true in the wild. No wonder we respond so eagerly when some travel agency tantalizes us with hints of a more "real" Alaska. Nature still holds out some hope of providing a genuine article, something that stands defiantly independent of our terminally ambiguous lives.

I assume that this need, this urge to get through the haze of our misunderstandings and see the real thing, is why we labor so mightily to test our very concept of the wild—why we persist in chipping away at the edges of our value judgments. We can't help ourselves. We are uneasy with past notions of perfection, and a place as sensational and easily loved as Brooks is ripe for modern cynicism. We object that nothing can be that good, and we get a little smug when we prove that it isn't. We feel compelled to point out that those bears probably didn't always behave just as they do now, or that we have had too simple an idea of wilderness, or that, in my case, when I catch one of these salmon, I may not be honoring my sporting code quite as fully as I imagined. If scientists cannot measure something without changing it, neither do we seem able to love it without effect. The irony of our love of nature is that we seem unable to exercise it without reducing the very qualities we treasure.

Nature, even modified nature with its wildness constrained or diminished, does not share our worry. That is precisely why it is so priceless, but it is also why we are on our own and must constantly decide what we will settle for and what will most do justice to our dreams.

Kurt Vonnegut asserted that "we are here on Earth to fart around. Don't let anybody tell you any different." But I wonder. In a differently valued world, this manipulative passion we feel, this compulsion to poke at things—to investigate and question and revise—might be a little embarrassing. I am sure that there are already people who believe that it is enough that Brooks River exists and we don't even need to see it to benefit from it in the finest way. To holders of this view, it isn't just fishing that is unnecessary; it's everything that gets in the way of nature's unmanipulated trajectory along this river. What is authentic and important here is unencumbered evolutionary intention, which we see as something purer and higher than anything we find elsewhere in our pursuit of wisdom.

It should be no surprise to us that such an unintrusive view might emerge. In the past few centuries of our relationship with nature, the tendency seems to be to ask, "How can you *do* that?" about progressively more things. Perhaps we really are headed in the direction so dreaded by the more heavy-handed nature enthusiasts—the trail bikers and shooters and flightseers and latter-day Crocketts for whom nature isn't worth it if they can't engage in a little creative violence. Perhaps eventually we will decide that remote adoration can be as fulfilling as what I do with my camera, binoculars, and fly rods. This seems sterile to me now, but someday other people may decide it's time. Until then, holding up such a prospect as a self-challenging part of our ideal—as a reminder of what the human spirit is capable of—wouldn't do us any harm.

But I'm not ready yet. I already do a lot of my nature appreciation from physical and emotional distances, and though I find it more valuable than I could ever express, it is not enough. At such distances I am like Haines's trapper, for whom "something is always withheld" and something "remains other and beyond." So I will keep going out to the trails to walk among the other, and maybe I will get close enough now and then to aim my binoculars at the near slopes of the beyond. I will go to the hills to watch, and to the rivers to search and reach and hope. And if my need for frequent reacquaintance with the real and my reliance on the technological crutches of binoculars and books and fly rods and cameras and words makes me a lesser pilgrim, at least I'm still out there, and I do think I'm getting better at it.

EPILOGUE

I write this in January. It's been more than a year since I left Alaska, a much longer time than I thought it would take me to decide if I would write about it and what I might like to say. Whenever I stop my work and go down to the kitchen to make a cup of hot chocolate, I celebrate the treat with a few minutes of passive absorption in the Yellowstone scene. I come back to my office, pull the window shade all the way up, rest my elbows on the frame, and look across the snow-covered flats between park service headquarters and the steaming lower terraces of Mammoth Hot Springs. There is a lot of snow, but it's getting old, and the sage and rabbitbrush that poke up through it are bare and dry.

Yesterday a few elk cows were resting in the shallower snow under the junipers near the springs. Today they must be somewhere else, but a magpie drops with a lazy flip of its tail from a low branch to the shadowed ground below, and I am reminded of how often I've seen that same easy little drop when it landed the bird on a fresh carcass. I wonder briefly if there's an early winterkill sheltered in the brush out there, but reject the thought and wonder instead if a tourist has left a sandwich unguarded on the ground. Always things to see, always matters to wonder on.

Early one morning late last fall, before the snow came to stay, I was fishing a local river that hosts an irregular spawning run of brown trout. These fish come up out of bigger water, energized and single-minded in their pursuit of procreation. They will almost certainly not meet a bear on this stream, though on other Yellowstone streams, spawning trout meet

215

quite a few. Here they will meet the occasional osprey or eagle, perhaps an otter once in a while, and me, flailing away with my fly rod in search of the connection that requires such constant renewal. My recurrent tendinitis—fly-caster's elbow—was at its worst in fifteen years. Every cast was a new opportunity for grating pain, and as much as I wanted to be there, I was a little relieved that it was the last day of the season.

The sun was not up. The river glowed in an undulating silver reflection of the predawn light—what Thoreau called "sky water." Between luminous sky and the mirroring river, the landscape was a dull, undifferentiated silhouette. Once I grimaced my way through the cast, I was almost a spectator as the heavy fly plopped up against the opposite bank of the run and made its long, swinging inquiries down the current.

It was fairly quiet until the end of the run, where the water broadened and shoaled before draining into a fishless gravel riffle. Just where depth and hope fade, a fish took the fly in midswing. It was not a big fish, about fourteen inches long, but it had the strength and pull of a giant, strong even for these metabolically supercharged spawners. Every two or three years I encounter one of these exceptional fish, like representatives of a higher race of animals. In their obviously superior power, they make me wonder why eventually they don't come to dominate the species. It jumped, then raced from one side of the stream to the other. Then, closer, it jumped again and came down flatly onto the river with a familiar and authoritative smack, and just for an instant I was back at Brooks River, feeling the rod buck and strain to the pull of a prodigal salmon and absorbing the warm shock of taking effect at such splendid distances.

The trout jerked me back to Wyoming. This was still a life-and-death struggle, no matter how far I had drifted in recognition and remembrance. When it was tired enough, I drew it in and lifted it into clear view in the gathering light and saw that shimmering beauty that, wherever I find it, seems like the most perfect thing I have ever seen, and that I turn from with a slight twinge of dread that this is the last time I will find it. Already and again, I am waiting for Alaska.

ACKNOWLEDGMENTS

I attempt to acknowledge my appreciation to Bob Barbee, Bill Pierce, Karen Gustin, and our other National Park Service hosts in Katmai in my story. I especially thank Jim Gavin and Tom Ferguson for their generous hospitality, and Bill Allen, Monte and Sue Crooks, and Mark Wagner for taking time to explain and introduce Brooks and Katmai to us. I also thank several Brooks fishermen, who I knew only briefly, either by their first names or only as the guy standing next to me, for their unfailing generosity with advice, encouragement, and split shot.

Many people provided me with information, publications, or guidance in my search for various documents. With the National Park Service, they included Terry DeBruyn (Anchorage), Ted Birkedal (Anchorage), Karen Gustin (Katmai), Deb Liggett (Katmai), Bess Lloyd (Denali), Sue Mills (Anchorage), Frank Norris (Anchorage), Jeanne Schaaf (Anchorage), Jane Tranel (Denali), Mark Wagner (Katmai), Jennifer Whipple (Yellowstone), and Lee Whittlesey (Yellowstone). Frank Norris's help was especially appreciated, as I barraged him with repeated and ever-more-detailed questions. In my travels around Alaska, personnel at several offices of the Alaska Fish and Game Department were consistently helpful. Kara Hartmann, with Friends of Katmai, and Chris Servheen, U.S. Fish and Wildlife Service, answered questions and provided publications as well.

The staffs of several libraries were of great assistance: ARLISS, Anchorage, Alaska; Denali National Park and Preserve Collection, Denali National Park, Alaska; Montana State

University Library, Bozeman, Montana; Technical Information Center, Denver, Colorado; Yellowstone Park Research Library, Yellowstone Park, Wyoming.

The manuscript was read and commented on by Rick Balkin, Bob Barbee, Marsha Karle, Sue Mills, and Frank Norris. As always, my agent Rick Balkin provided his usual fine guidance. And the folks at Stackpole Books saw it through the publication process with their customary grace and care; I especially thank Mark Allison, Amy Hixon, and Joyce Bertsch for their attention to the book's needs.

As this book was about to go to press, my brother-in-law and friend Bill Karle, a lifelong outdoorsman who loved wildlife and wild country, died suddenly and much too soon. I celebrate his life and his memory by dedicating *Real Alaska* to him. He would have loved Katmai.

READINGS AND SOURCES

$\mathbf{M}$ost of what has been written about Katmai has appeared in magazines, government reports, or in scientific journals; very few popular books have been written about the area. Perhaps the most sought-after of these is Robert Griggs, *The Valley of Ten Thousand Smokes* (Washington, DC: National Geographic Society, 1922), a handsome, well-illustrated book that combines the information from a number of earlier *National Geographic* articles and is a classic of Alaskan exploration literature. Equally desirable and perhaps even more entertaining is Victor Cahalane, *A Biological Survey of Katmai National Monument* (Washington, DC: Smithsonian Institution, 1959), which is more than worth owning just for the wonderful long chapter on bears. Both the Griggs and Cahalane books are hard to come by, but are available through interlibrary loan, as are the following titles.

The two essential volumes for understanding the history and literature of Katmai National Park and Preserve are John Hussey, *Embattled Katmai: A History of Katmai National Monument* (San Francisco: National Park Service, 1971), and Frank Norris, *Isolated Paradise: An Administrative History of the Katmai and Aniakchak National Park Units* (Anchorage, AK: National Park Service, 1996). Both of these superb works were published in very small editions and are essentially out of print. Hussey devoted proportionately more attention to the Katmai region prior to the creation of the national monument, while Norris provides the most detailed account of the administrative history of the monument, park, and preserve. Both are exhaustively documented—they are genuine bibliographical treasures for the person who wants to track down more details of the story. A fine companion volume that focuses on historic sites and resources is Janet Clemens and Frank Norris, *Building in an Ashen Land: Katmai National Park and Preserve Historic Resource Study* (Anchorage, AK: National Park Service, 1999). Like the Hussey and Norris titles, this was also produced in a small edition.

Two locally published books provide good overviews of Katmai attractions. Jean Bodeau's *Katmai National Park and Preserve, Alaska* (Anchorage, AK: Alaska Natural History Association, 1996) is a thoughtful and trustworthy introductory guidebook for the visitor who might have interest in hiking, fishing, camping, and other activities in the park. Tamara Olson and Ronald Squibb, *Brown Bears of Brooks River* (Kodiak, AK: Squibb, 1993), is a handsome twenty-four-page, full-color celebration of the bears, informed by the authors' research and enhanced by James Gavin's beautiful photographs.

Dave Bohn's *Rambles through an Alaskan Wild: Katmai and the Valley of the Smokes* (Santa Barbara, CA: Capra Press, 1979) is a lovely photo essay with Bohn's provocative personal narrative, which I recommend for its strong impressions and stronger opinions. It was printed in an edition of five thousand and is available locally.

There are, of course, many other publications that deal with Katmai. But a number of government reports are certainly of book size and deserving of attention. For the purposes of my book, I found great value and illumination in the 576-page *Final Development Concept Plan, Environmental Impact Statement, Brooks River Area, Katmai National Park and Preserve, Alaska* (Denver: National Park Service, 1996). It is in government documents such as this that one can taste all the flavors of public opinion that arise in the management of important lands.

The following bibliography is limited to items quoted, cited, or otherwise mentioned in the text.

Alaska Department of Fish and Game. *1998 Sport Fishing Regulations Summary, North Gulf Coast, Upper Copper and Upper Susitna River Drainages.* Juneau, AK: Alaska Department of Fish and Game, 1998.

Beach, Rex. *The Silver Horde.* New York: Harper & Brothers Publishers, 1909.

Birkedal, Ted. "Ancient Hunters in the Alaskan Wilderness: Human Predators and Their Role and Effect on Wildlife Populations and the Implications for Resource Management." *Seventh Conference on Research & Resource Management in Parks and on Public Lands: Partners in Stewardship,* November 16–20, 1992, Jacksonville, Florida. George Wright Society, (1993): 228–234.

Bohn, Dave. *Rambles through an Alaskan Wild: Katmai and the Valley of the Smokes.* Santa Barbara, CA: Capra Press, 1979.

Cahalane, Victor. *A Biological Survey of Katmai National Monument.* Washington, DC: Smithsonian Institution, 1959.

Chadwick, Douglas. "Grizz: Of Men and the Great Bear." *National Geographic* 169, no. 2 (February 1986): 182–213.

Chaucer, Geoffrey. *The Canterbury Tales.* Oxford: Oxford University Press, 1985.

Claar, James, and Paul Schullery, eds. *Bears: Their Biology and Management.* Papers from the Ninth International Conference on Bear Research and Management, Missoula, Montana, February 23–28, 1992. Yellowstone National Park: International Association for Bear Research and Management/Yellowstone Center for Resources, 1994.

Craighead, Charles. *Images of Nature: The Photographs of Thomas D. Mangelsen.* Southport, CT: Levin Associates, 1989.

Deloria, Vine, Jr. *Red Earth, White Lies: Native Americans and the Myth of Scientific Fact.* New York: Scribner, 1995.

Denver, John. "To the Wild Country." Port Chester, NY: Cherry Lane Music Company, 1971.

Dinesen, Isak. *Out of Africa.* New York: Vintage, 1985.

Doto, Pamela. "Ornery Bear Nips Ranger in Katmai." *Anchorage Daily News* (July 26, 1991): B1.

Ferrell, Ed. *Strange Stories of Alaska and the Yukon.* Fairbanks, AK: Epicenter Press, 1996.

Griggs, Robert. "The Valley of Ten Thousand Smokes: An Account of the Discovery and Exploration of the Most Wonderful Volcanic Region in the World." *National Geographic* 33, no. 2 (February 1918): 115–69.

———. "Our Greatest National Monument." *National Geographic* 30, no. 3 (September 1921): 219–92.

———. "The Vegetation of Katmai District." *Ecology* 17, no. 3 (July 1936): 380–417.

Haines, John. *The Stars, the Snow, the Fire.* St. Paul, MN: Graywolf Press, 1989.

Hartmann, Kara. "Friends of Katmai: A Public Relations Campaign to Establish a National Park Advocacy Organization." M.S. thesis, University of Utah, Salt Lake City, 1998.

Heinrich, Bernd. *Ravens in Winter.* New York: Summit Books, 1989.

Herrero, Stephen. *Bear Attacks: Their Causes and Avoidance.* New York: Nick Lyons Books, 1985.

Hickel, Wally. "Building on the Fault Zone." In Ron Strickland, ed., *Alaskans: Life on the Last Frontier.* Harrisburg, PA: Stackpole Books, 1992.

Holzworth, John. *The Wild Grizzlies of Alaska.* New York: G. P. Putnam's Sons, 1930.

Hubbard, Bernard. *Cradle of Storms.* New York: Dodd, Mead and Company, 1935.

Huckabee, John. Letter to David Graber, July 23, 1987, National Park Service, Sequoia Kings Canyon National Park. National Park Service Alaska Support Office files, Anchorage, Alaska.

Jans, Nick. *The Last Light Breaking: Living among Alaska's Inupiat Eskimos.* Anchorage, AK: Alaska Northwest Books, 1993.

Jefferson, Thomas. *Notes on the State of Virginia.* New York: Harper & Row, 1964.

Kent, Rockwell. *Wilderness: A Journal of Quiet Adventure in Alaska.* Hanover, NH: Wesleyan University Press, 1996.

Kerasote, Ted. *Heart of Home.* New York: Villard, 1997.

Krech, Shepard, III. *The Ecological Indian, Myth and History.* New York: W. W. Norton & Company, 1999.

L'Amour, Louis. *Jubal Sackett.* New York: Bantam, 1985.

Large, Arlen. "Lewis & Clark Meet the American Incognitum.'" *We Proceeded On* (journal of the Lewis and Clark Trail Heritage Foundation) (August 1995): 12–18.

Lopez, Barry. *Arctic Dreams.* New York: Charles Scribner's Sons, 1986.

McClenahan, Patricia. "National Register of Historic Places, Registration Form, Brooks River Archeological District." National Park Service Alaska Regional Office, Anchorage, Alaska, March 24, 1989.

Muir, John. *Travels in Alaska.* New York: Penguin, 1993.

Murie, Adolph. *The Grizzlies of Mount McKinley.* Washington, DC: U.S. Government Printing Office, 1981.

Murie, Olaus. *Fauna of the Aleutian Islands and the Alaska Peninsula.* Washington, DC: U.S. Fish and Wildlife Service/U.S. Government Printing Office, 1969.

———. *Journeys to the Far North.* Palo Alto, CA: Wilderness Society and American West Publishing Company, 1973.

National Park Service. "Conclusions and Recommendations Relevant to the Management of Bears and People at Brooks River, Katmai National Park, November 25, 1991." National Park Service Alaska Support Office files, Anchorage, Alaska, 1991.

————. *Bear Facts.* Anchorage, AK: Alaska Natural History Association, 1997 and 1998.

Olson, Tamara, and Barrie Gilbert. "Variable Impacts of People on Brown Bear Use of an Alaskan River." *International Conference on Bear Research and Management* 9, no. 1 (1994): 97–106.

Olson, Jack. *Night of the Grizzlies.* New York: Signet Books, 1969.

Pike, Warburton. *Through the Subarctic Forest.* London: Edward Arnold, 1896.

Rolston, Holmes. "Biology and Philosophy in Yellowstone." *Biology and Philosophy* 5 (1990): 241–58.

Russell, Andy. *Grizzly Country.* New York: Alfred Knopf, 1967.

Sagan, Carl. *Pale Blue Dot.* New York: Random House, 1994.

Schullery, Paul. "A Reasonable Illusion." *Rod and Reel* 5 (November–December 1979): 44–54.

————. *The Bears of Yellowstone.* 3rd ed. Worland, WY: High Plains Publishing Company, 1992.

————. *Searching for Yellowstone: Ecology and Wonder in the Last Wilderness.* Boston: Houghton Mifflin Company, 1997.

Schoen, John, and Christopher Servheen. "Comments on the Management Issues at Brooks Camp, Katmai National Park." Report to Regional Director Robert Barbee, National Park Service Alaska Regional Office, Anchorage, Alaska, July 23, 1998.

Sheldon, Charles. *The Wilderness of Denali.* New York: Charles Scribner's Sons, 1930.

Singer, Frank. "Review of Case Incident Reports: Bear Incidents, March 19, 1982." National Park Service Alaska Support Office files, Anchorage, Alaska.

Steinbeck, John. *Travels with Charley*. New York: The Viking Press, 1962.

Straley, John. *The Woman Who Married a Bear*. New York: Signet, 1994.

Thomas, Jack Ward. "From Managing a Deer Herd to Moving a Mountain: One Pilgrim's Progress." *Journal of Wildlife Management* 64, no. 1 (2000): 1–10.

Troyer, Will. "Distribution and Densities of Brown Bear on Various Streams in Katmai National Monument." National Park Service Alaska Area Office, Anchorage, Alaska, 1980.

Vonnegut, Kurt. *Timequake*. New York: G. P. Putnam's Sons, 1997.

Walker, Tom, and Larry Aumiller. *The Way of the Grizzly*. Stillwater, MN: Voyagers Press, 1993.

Whitney, David. "Brooks Camp Relocation Pulled from Budget." *Anchorage Daily News* (October 13, 1999): B1.

Wilson, President Woodrow. "A Proclamation." No. 1487, September 24, 1918, 40 Stat. 1885.

"Wrong Volcano Blamed." *Science News Letter* 69 (April 21, 1956): 246.

Yukon Department of Renewable Resources. "Sport Fishing Regulations Summary, 1998–1999." Whitehorse, Yukon Territory, 1998.